The Soul tha...
for attention, is like
"A Mischievous Child"

How to
Love Yourself
Back
to
Power

DIVINE ⫸ HOUSE
B O O K S

ISBN: 978-0-578-85801-2

Possibilities and Impossibilities "are both offsprings" of how we view the validity of our own existence in this world! They are not "handed" to YOU from another! YOU do have the permission to BE "whatever YOU are ready to endure!"

Undrai Fizer
The 365: A Personal Compass to Self Discovery & Enlightenment

Contents

Definitions 1

Language of the Soul 7

Listen to Your Soul... 25

Recognizing Self-Embarrassment... 41

Where Is Home? 49

The Actual Experience.. 58

Restores.... 67

Recognizing the Aura of Your Presence 74

Have YOU Determined Your Healer? 83

Our Healing Creates Assignments for Us 96

Authenticity Cannot Lie! 100

Anticipation. Closing on The Life.... 110

Who We Are Will Let Us Know 116

DEFINITIONS

mis·chie·vous | \ ˈmis-chə-vəs 🔊,
ˈmish-; *nonstandard* mis-ˈchē-vē-əs 🔊,
mish- \

Definition of *mischievous*

1 : <u>HARMFUL</u>, <u>INJURIOUS</u>
// mischievous gossip

2   **a**   : able or tending to cause
annoyance, trouble, or minor
injury

      b   : irresponsibly playful
// mischievous behavior

🔊   **mis·chie·vous**
/ˈmisCHivəs/

adjective

(of a person, animal, or their behavior)
causing or showing a fondness for causing
trouble in a playful way.
"two mischievous kittens had decorated the
bed with shredded newspaper"

Similar: (naughty) (bad) (⌄)

- (of an action or thing) causing or intended
  to cause harm or trouble.
  "a mischievous allegation for which there is
  not a shred of evidence"

Similar: (malicious) (malevolent) (⌄)

1

When we see or hear of the term "mischievous," what comes to mind? Regardless of the definitions that you read, how does your heart perceive the term? Now, imagine a vital part of our lives responding and reacting this way. Imagine our very own Soul acting as a little, mischievous child. Have you ever perceived your Soul to be an actual Person? Have you recognized the actual Personhood of YOU? I know that you know that you are a person, yes. But have you recognized "the kind" of Being that YOU are? You are very well aware of your sensitivities, feelings, and personality. But do YOU know how your Soul perceives YOU? Do you know how the Image that YOU were created in, perceives YOU. Do you know how your very Presence perceives YOU? YOU are looking at YOU, everyday and you may not even realize it. I am not writing this book from a clinical or psychological vantage point. I am not a clinical psychologist. I am not a medical doctor, even though I've earned a Ph.D. in Humanities, which is a type of cultural anthropology and the study of human and religious behavior. YOU are not obligated to believe and accept my findings. YOU are not obligated to totally agree with all of the content in this book. But I do know that YOU will find yourself, somewhere, in these pages. YOU will read something that totally speaks to the core thought and rhythm of your heart. I do believe this. YOU may not agree with much of the terminology. Yet, you will see beyond the terminology, for your heart will move when you connect with a certain vibe within the conversation. We can find ourselves within everyone. We are all divinely connected together from the Divine Source that determined our ways and means. We can always find ourselves in all of our Selves. We are a very peculiar people, *(I Peter 2:9, the Scriptures)*.

Can you imagine your Soul treating YOU in a mischievous way? Can you imagine your very own Consciousness having a mind of its own, as well as desiring a relationship with YOU? Your Life is seeking a relationship with YOU. Your life desires to love you with all of its heart. These are the spiritual wonders that we have not realized about ourselves.

The Wisdom of God has intertwined Love within the core fabric of our Being. Love is within us, as us, loving us continually through our imagination, Spirit, and mind. Love is reaching out for us all the time. But when we deny ourselves, we will not see it. We become busy looking for others to give love to us, without realizing that we are denying the Love that is already being given to us, through God, within us. Imagine your Soul acting mischievously with YOU. What are the things that YOU think "your mischievous child" is doing with you or has already done with YOU? What are the ugly and annoying things that you believe has taken place with YOU? A mischievous soul is one of life's greatest enemies and annoyances. The Soul however, is a beautiful thing. It's simply reaching out to YOU for love. You have not been listening to your "child." YOU may have been too busy to recognize the fact that the pain YOU are feeling is not coming from loneliness, or the need of companionship. This Pain is coming from your Soul, so desperately desiring your attention. Your Soul desires to uncover more beautiful things within YOU. Your Soul wants to be your friend. Listen for it. Listen to it. You will see what I'm talking about.

We are fearfully and wonderfully made,
(Psalm 139:14, The Scriptures).

We are a daily, living wonder of God. Your Body is the Temple of the Living God. YOU, as a temple, are a moving house of Glory. But if this truth does not produce fulfillment, it will not satisfy the heart. Your heart finds happiness in what it is yearning for you. A Soul that lacks attention from its Possessor, will seek to "drive your life" to the place it desires to go. Your Soul may be responsible for many of the "mishaps" you have faced in life. It is acting uncontrollable and miserable, simply because it is not experiencing Love from YOU. You are not seeing it. Your Soul feels invisible to YOU and it is screaming for you to open your eyes! God has strategically designed us not to lose. We are not designed to go astray. We are designed to respond to the unction of our Soul. In the unction, resides the Power and the Solution. We are divinely designed to answer the call of our Divine Unction. We are not designed to permanently "fail!" We are not designed to dissipate. We are an Eternal Substance of the Divine. But when we fail to recognize this relevance, we become "mere human beings" to ourselves.

YOU are more than You've realized. However, your Soul has "deemed" you as a problem within yourself. It has caused you to perceive yourself as a burden, and you are waiting to see how long your "relationships are going to last!" YOU are busy "changing yourself" in order to fit in with the others. YOU also feel that it's not fair for you to "do all of the changing," while others remain themselves. But this isn't their fault. It's yours. When you don't know yourself, you're living a non-authentic life. You're trying to mimic what seems acceptable, but you are missing the substance of the heart. You're trying to fit in spaces "you know nothing about!" You are also using anger and comparison to others to be your fuel to inspiration and change. When anger is used for Change, it simply establishes you as an "anger agent," and not a transformative power. Whatever it is that is responsible for changing you, is the exact thing that's going to propel YOU. Even if its negative. When anger and disappointment are the instruments that dictated your "shift in life," you will find yourself constantly attracting these things to your Life. Remember this, because you're going to read it again further in this book. Whatever it is that is responsible for having you in this place, are the exact things that you continue to attract to your Life. Unless you're ready for something authentic and new!

LANGUAGE OF
THE SOUL

Can you imagine your very own soul; and core expression of who you really are, "playfully or annoyingly," misplacing your inner-peace and joy of living and becoming? Can you imagine the innate "ugliness" that our very own soul will exude as a result of living within ourselves, without fully celebrating and honoring The Divine Presence of ourselves, in the world? When the Soul seeks profound attention and nurturing from ourselves, it will act "as a mischievous" child, "knocking over dishes of purpose, misplacing our confidence and hiding them within our fears and false expectations, while lying about us in our very own minds, causing us to lose confidence within ourselves. When we ignore the Powers that awaken within us, as a result of taking the bold step of honoring our relevance in the world, the Soul will take it upon itself, to "remind us" that we forgetting to prepare our inner offspring of the governance that it was designed for, before the foundations of the world.

We are creative byproducts of the most confident, bold, Divine Spirit of the Universe. We are the offspring of The Unlimited Kind. We are all, significant and relevant expressions of The Living God. This Reality has no religion. This Reality is empowered by LOVE. This Reality fully embraces itself and in its Divine Preeminence, "fears no failure." There is no competition with it. We are the images of Love, designed from Love, and powered by Love. I could write all of the words of Christ while seeking to establish an intellectual or theological argument from which to base my findings. But this would be to no avail. For a change, we must be first recover our capacity to respond to the hidden languages of the Soul. Many things we consider to be psychological or clinical, yes. But there is a core language, hidden deep within the confines of Consciousness, that speaks loudest through our behavior, thought, and confidence.

Our soul speaks perpetually. It rapidly sends signals of energy which establishes a perception of who we are during any given situation or circumstance. Through each shift of life, we perceive who we are, quickly and silently. We get a simple taste of our own influence and control through everything. And usually, we find that we are "nothing." We get a glimpse of what our lives truly mean to us, others, and maybe even the world around us. We get a sense of how the Atmosphere relates to our existence, time, hope, and mind. Will Hope respond to us? As a matter of fact, I want to know if Hope actually sees me as a viable person? Will Hope help me? Am I being seen and loved? When we have yet to comprehend our soul's love language, it will cause us to be denied of the Clarity of Spirit that we so desperately need. We have grown accustomed to using relationships as "silent gauges" and "measurements" of validation. Instead of loving the simple powers found in mutual growth and oneness, we use them to measure our own importance, while "keeping score" of how each person responds to our ills, disappointments, and circumstances. We keep score on how many calls were received between one another, and visits to one another, as well as how much empathy was shown towards the tragedies of our lives. Each person measures how they are personally responded to during times of crisis. We begin to evaluate and measure the significance of our own, personal relevance, through the actions of those we "respect!" This can evolve into a depressing, downward spiral of the soul.

It is a dangerous thing to put the entire relevance of your existence, into the hands of others and their own response to your life. Many live for the validating reactions of another instead of living in response to the Love of their very own Soul. Your Soul desires for you to live for no one else but its Love. Many take their own lives, simply because others have rejected the relevance of their Lives. The "mischievous" Consciousness "annoyingly HID their confidence through a myriad of problems, issues, and trials, NOT BECAUSE IT HATED THEM, BUT BECAUSE IT WAS MISSING THE PERSON'S PRESENCE!" When our soul misses time in our Presence, it will act accordingly. The tragic thing with many, is that they don't realize how important they really are to their Soul.

We live in a world of comparison amongst copies. Originality is frowned upon because it has no precedent before it. Originality is designed to embrace the full, brunt of misunderstanding, mis-judgement, and criticism. When it is the first, there are no comparisons. One must be authentically bold to be FIRST. To live without precedent. To live without the acceptable sphere of measurement that we have grown accustomed to. This is a major key in loving ourselves BACK TO POWER! The Power is not in how your surroundings will respond to your Difference in Peace, but it's how YOU WILL PEACEFULLY RESPOND TO YOUR OWN EXISTENCE!

How do you respond to your existence? What does your own Presence inspire YOU to do? The soul recognizes when its Presence is mutually respected between YOU and your Behavior. The soul knows when it's being compelled, or forced, to compare itself to another. It despises being compared, and it hates not being believed in and known. Have YOU ever recognized the Person-ship of Your very own Soul? Did you think your soul was "a smoky haze of formless matter" that simply floats around within your body? Did you perceive the Soul has being a spiritual play on words? Did you know that your Soul has ideas, and is a Designer's Original of Pure Intent? Do you even know that your soul is in a relationship with you? Have you yet discerned that what you are desiring to receive from another "is the same energies that your soul is desiring to receive from YOU?" The feelings you have in thinking that "others don't understand YOU," are the same feelings your soul is interjecting towards YOU! Your Soul is thinking through YOU "while you're perceiving that it's a reaction to YOU from the outside world!" We are waiting and yearning for love from outside of us, while our Soul is waiting for Love from within us!

The tragic truth is that we don't feel that we matter in a profound way. If we did, we would respond to ourselves with powerful energy and intention. We procrastinate with every place, person, or thing that we aren't ready to arrive for; better yet, early. If we truly loved ourselves, we will naturally show up for ourselves. ON TIME and IN TIME! The mischievousness activities of the Soul reveals that it is seeking authentic attention from YOU. If you are inwardly embarrassed in the fact that YOU can love yourself, you will not pay attention to the brilliance of your mind. If we are ashamed of ourselves in some innate way, we will not pay attention to the relevance of our lives. We will silently despise our lives, while "blocking out" the events of past shame and situations. We will be blind to the fact that our soul has not experienced this personal shame that yet resonates within your memory. We are not fully comprehending that our Soul perceives us as the Perfect Specimen of Life, and that it is inspiring us to do beautiful things, simply because we are beautiful in its eyes!

Your Soul thinks that you're beautiful and full of wonder. It's telling you this every day. Are you paying attention to it? When we ignore the brilliant promptings of our Soul, we depress it to the point that it will react through our behavior and personality. It will "inspire" us to break up much needed relationships, while sabotaging networks of Purpose, through petty misunderstandings. The mischievousness of the soul will "misplace" the Clarity that has within it, the Power to awaken every dimension of one's mind. It will "hide it" in another memory, hoping that YOU would look within to recover it. But why seek out things "through irrelevant boxes?" When you feel that within YOU is nothing, you will not search there! When we do not feel important in our own Presence, we won't look for importance to be there. We will look for it through another. Or, we will trust ourselves in finding someone else who has the brilliance, and credit ourselves for finding them. Have YOU once gave credit to yourself for finding YOU?

In my experience, I began to resolve the inferiority complexes within myself once I began to make peace with myself. When I began to make peace with Me, being an intentional Divine Idea from God, my Soul began to "uncover all of the hidden places that stored my confidence, creativity, and Purpose!" It was with me all the time, but hidden within the "houses of inner-misperception and fears of failure!" When we exist, while paying the mortgages of hidden houses of failure, we invoke the fears of launching out into the Deep! We fear beginning, even though our lives are being tempted with brilliant ideas. We spend time preparing for our fears of crashing, instead of the Power found in Flying! We spend years making our lives "crash proof," simply because we yearn for the respect of others to keep us in the air! When I began to make peace with my Soul, it encouraged me to take the leap of Divine Faith! It compelled to me jump after myself, in the Oceans of Divine Knowing!" I leaped after myself. It affirmed that my "pilot's license would not be revoked if I crashed!" The significance of my Knowing would not be revoked if I landed awkwardly. I would not be rejected if my idea did not work. I would not be a failure "if my dream failed!" The more that I began to make peace with Me, I became a vessel of Peace. And my soul stopped playing tricks on ME! I was able to keep myself in the air, even when Life "forced down my craft!" My Soul is with me. Loving me always.

It takes Power in loving yourself back to Prominence. YOU must do more than believe it. YOU must KNOW IT! Your Soul is constantly telling you what you know. But are YOU choosing to "believe" something else? Are you allowing your own memories to defeat YOU? Are you requiring feelings of comparison to affirm YOU? Are you fulfilled by your Presence? Or, are you merely satisfied with yourself? Fulfillment is an experience with the yearning of your Soul. It means that you've encountered it, without hindrance. It has Solved your questionings and wanderings.

Fulfillment is more than an answer. It is the Solution. To many, The Kingdom is merely an answer, but it isn't the Solution. Oneness with my Self, and my Divine Reality, was the actual, authentic solution for my soul's torment. To many, however, it may not be close. We all innately seek and pursue what our heart is yearning for. We feel that if we get it, our wanderings will cease. When we misunderstand our Divine Identity, it will appear to merely be a religious experience that has yet to solve the mischievousness of our Soul. A religious experience will still "hide our Powerful, Self-Discoveries of Oneness" with the verses of Scripture, while yet leaving us with no Inner-Standing on how to celebrate ourselves back to Power!

How does your reality respond to the fact that you are an offspring of the Greatest Spirit and Mind in all of Time? How do you innately react to the fact that YOU are already total Brilliance and Light in the world? How do YOU naturally respond to this Truth, beyond the theological rhetoric of spirituality? Are YOU responding to your talent, or your Presence? Are you reacting to the reactions of others, who are responding to YOU? Are you responding to the comparisons, or being Original?

When you make Peace with The Person of the Divine YOU, your Soul will begin *to "restore all of the years that the locust had eaten, the canker-worm, and the caterpillar, and the palmer-worm, my great army that I sent among YOU!" (Joel 2:25, The Scriptures)*

Your Soul will give back everything it hidden from YOU as a result of desperately seeking after Your attention, honor, and love. Your Soul is the Divine Reality that resonates within YOU. Within it, resides all of the Brilliance and Beauty of your Being! Your Soul only "hid" them in order to find YOU. Your Soul wanted YOU to find it, in all the Powers of your Love. When we find no fulfillment with us, when we are not the Solutions to our yearning, we will look for another. We must become more than an option for ourselves. We must become the Solution. If not, we will be tormented by the fillings of satisfaction, which is but a convenient alternative to the wanderings. We will be full, while yet "seeking for more!"

When we lack honor for our Presence, we also lack honor for the Presence of God! God is not only with us, God is being US, with US. Through US. And to US. Our Soul rejoices in this truth and reality. Our Soul is yearning for agreement in this Reality with us. Our Soul seeks partnership with us. It desires to grow and manifest Power together, from the Root of this Divine Reality! What we are knowing about us, will empower us to Celebrate ourselves as offspring of Unlimited Love.

Our Soul is empowering us with our reasons for Being! We are not here for "a work." We are here, in the world, from the reality of LOVE. We are not here to simply do things. LOVE and LIGHT, produced us. How another "celebrates" our work, does not lengthen our years. It does not provide fulfilling influence. Your Soul is celebrating YOU always. Do you sense it? Can YOU feel it?

How we commune with our Soul is a direct result of how we commune with our own Influence. Our own knowing of our Perfect Self. The way we respond, without shame to ourselves, will determine how we "leap into ourselves!" We don't merely "speak" to our Soul. We live confidently from the Influence that we celebrate through our Lives.

We are loving ourselves back to Original Power. We are establishing Peace with ourselves, as well as experiencing the recovery of all things previously "hidden!"

We will no longer judge ourselves out of Power. As we celebrate our existence, by way of going against the grain of our "memories of defeat," we will establish an Original Truth to Power. When we judge ourselves out of Power, we are innately calling ourselves hypocrites for thinking "beauty," while existing "ugly!" It is the reality of the ego. We feel that if we produce something brilliant, the responses of others will deliver us out of the hole! The stronger the response, the greater the ego. The longer the response, the greater the cause. We find ourselves under an overwhelming pressure to perform, while silently losing our way back to Power. The pressures of the validation that we seek from lying to ourselves, has now become our new truth. The Soul is not designed to live from lies, so it will " begin to trash your surroundings" until YOU find your "Self!" When the Soul is angered or depressed, it will let YOU know. The Soul knows that YOU are reaching for the attention of another to keep you alive, while ignoring

The Tree of Life that is resonating on the inside of YOU! When we deny our own life, we find ourselves dying for the attention of another, until we actually die. By our own hands, or our own feelings of defeat.

Loving yourself back to Divine Relevance is as consistent as your Celebration. God cannot help us do what we do not desire to do. Your own consistency is as poweful as the love that you are loving YOU with. Consistency is the proof of Desire, Yearning, and Fulfillment. Consistency is the confirmation of the yearning encounter. I AM in the PRESENCE of what my Soul has been speaking about. I don't have to abandon it. Consistency is living and existing from the Fulfilling Experience, "and throwing away the key!" As long as I hold the key, I relish the flexibility of leaving when I desire. If I am yet seeking for a greater opportunity, my present condition is only temporary. LOVE is the fulfillment and the Solution. But as I stated before, to many, it is but a mere answer.

The Soul knows the difference between a yearning fulfilled, and a convenient alternative. I am a result of an inner conflict that was solved. It restored my Soul. It calmed the annoyance within my being. Our degree of yearning is determined by the world we exist from. We, as Consciousness, exist from "our own, perceived realm of laws, needs, survival tools, and intuition." We are all citizens of a silent world within. In this world are found our "spiritual dogmas and comprehensions," and personal meanings of life. We function from who we think we are. Where we "are" determines "Where" we are. Where we exist in Consciousness, determines where we exist in the schemes of the world we live in. Where we "are" within us, determines what naturally invites itself towards us and within us. We perceive from the place "we are" in self-thought. Our worlds are framed by "the faith" we possess. When we exist from the Place of Comparison, Divine Reality will not solve our yearning. We can only yearn for the food that exist in the world we live from. Eternal Meat will not solve the yearning of those who live below it. It is an Answer, yes. But not a Solution. We seek the fruits of the world we live from most. The Soul does not seek a cordial or tolerable co-existence between worlds. Therefore, the Soul will constantly produce dissatisfaction and disturbances within our sphere of living, until we properly interpret what it is saying. It is compelling us to awaken to the Power of Recognizing the difference between Fulfillment and Satisfaction. Yearning vs. Convenience.

Do we feel that we deserve ourselves? We are the first-fruits of self-treatment. How we deserve ourselves will determine how we treat ourselves. Are we treating ourselves perfectly and with fulfillment? When our Soul respects us, it will stop annoying us with questions. It will refrain from playing with us when issues of Life are on the line. When problems arise, we will possess clear direction on what to create, instead of getting lost within the confusion of the moment. When our Soul has gained our truest attention, our Soul will release the prophetic clarity of Vision within us. It will lead us within, to every Place we are to go. Our Soul will assure us that we will not lose our way. We can powerfully and confidently engage in daily living, knowing that our "airport" will not lose its license to operate in the air of Purpose.

If you're going to do this, why not go all the way? Never

lower the bar for convenience. Fulfillment will naturally inspire YOU to go where the yearning can be solved. No matter how high the flight, or how deep the Ocean. You will navigate yourself to the Source of the Need. Have you determined the Source of your need, and not merely the rhetorical answer to your Need? We all go where our "needs are calling us!" Where are your needs calling YOU to? Through our "needs," we find what is God to us. Whatever is Lord to us, determines what and how we think of ourselves, as well as the world around us. Whatever is Lord to us, determines what masters us. Whatever is Lord to us, determines what we "allow" and how we naturally flow and engage in Life. Whatever is Lord to us, determines the Solutions, or the Answers, to our "needs!"

Have you realized what your Soul is letting You do? Have you realized whom the Soul perceives as its Lord, or master? Is your Soul causing YOU to be fearful of Light, or accepting of Light? When the Soul is in its mischievous state, clarity is hidden everywhere. When Clarity is hidden, fear is always present. When Clarity is hidden, even belief is nerving. Simply because fear is more tangible than the faith you are seeking to believe from. When the Soul is hurting, it will hide the tangible-ness of knowing right under the depressions of your memories. When Peace is hidden, fear is present. When we exist as mere members of the Earth, instead of relevant beings of The Divine Reality, we feel exposed to elements of the temporal world. We feel we are victims to the many whims of the Human Condition.

LISTEN TO
YOUR SOUL…

Years ago, while living on the Central Coast of California, my children and I rode out to a known computer store. I was going to replace a laptop that was "fried by accident" by my youngest son, Zion. While I left Zion at home with his mother, I took the two older sons, Benjamin and Loren, with me. As we sat in the parking lot, and as I rummaged through the receipts and paperwork, eagerly awaiting the replacement of my laptop, I didn't notice Loren's need for my attention. As he sat in his car seat, while fastened in the back area of the truck, he began to kick the driver side console very adamantly and consistently. I didn't even notice it at the time for I was "heavily engaged into getting my receipts together in order to replace a significant object of value." Did you get that? As a result of not paying attention to my son, he began to annoy me by kicking the console. When I finally realized what he was doing, I raised my voice in displeasure by saying to him, "What's wrong with you? Why are you sitting there just kicking the seat, Loren?" I didn't realize that he wasn't merely kicking the seat. He was seeking my attention. He wanted me to interpret a voice that he had not learned to verbalize. He wanted me to connect with his heart. He wanted me to nurture what he could not speak.

The Soul is just like our children. It desires for us to articulate the deeply embedded values of Power that resonate within us, but we have no words for it. We are disconnected from who we are, while being more connected to what we sense we are obligated to be. We are more in tune to what Life is demanding from us through poverty, than what we are to offer the world through love. The Soul will begin to make senseless noise within our Consciousness in order for us to make sense of the chaos we have become so tolerant of. Our Soul is not disturbing us just to annoy us. Our Soul is speaking something to us that our lives are too busy to understand. We are too busy dying, while living. It is time to listen to our Soul. It's time to listen to our Love. When is the last time you listened to your own Love?

Your Soul will reveal its love for YOU. It will let YOU know what it feels for YOU through strength, power, and continual, brilliant imagination. The Love of God will communicate to us through incredible imagination and the desire for uncommon exploits. The Brilliance of Wisdom will compel us to re-imagine ourselves in Greater Identity. The Vision of the Christ-Mind will inspire us to see ourselves in fullness, as well as the fullness of His Nature. Your Soul will begin to share stories with YOU. It will begin to rehearse the conversations it has waited for so long to have with YOU. When we go years, absent of conversation with the Soul, the agitation that the Soul will feel will seem unbearable. Sometimes, the "seasons of dryness and disappointments" in our lives, are not merely LIFE being LIFE. It is the Soul, suffering from feelings of abuse, neglect, and absence. It is the inner Purpose, of who we truly are, dying at the root, while yearning for our Conversation. Yes, our very own Purpose has a language of love. It desires to not only be written on "tablets of stone," but it desires to be conversed with from the heart. Deep calls unto Deep!

The Soul, when loved, will lead us back to Power. It will lead us back to Divine Originality and Governance. It will begin to uncover the hiding places that held all of our toys, lives, and joys, captive in the caves of despair, memories, broken relationships, and destroyed dreams. The Soul had nowhere else to go.

It had nowhere else to complain or to plead for justice on its behalf. Our Soul can become as stubborn as we are. Seeking to prove a point that is no longer relevant to be proven.

Vision are the stories that your Soul will share within your imagination. The Soul will shower us with possibilities, compelling us to take on the "identity of its very own Maker!" The Soul will open the doors of Becoming to us. It will invite us, in every moment, to become the Great Person that we have feared to be all of our lives. We were too embarrassed to BE this Person. We've established too many accidents in life to be given the keys legitimately. Our memories are holding us hostage. Our doubts are holding us hostage. And the sad truth is also this, "the people we respect" are holding us hostage, too! We can't seem to override the opinions of those we truly respect, even though "they" aren't doing anything ill towards us!

I have found that I cannot love anyone else greater than I love myself. If I am loving YOU, while despising me, then I am not loving YOU. I am loving "an idea of love." I am not loving. I am admiring the ideas of what love could be. But I am not loving anything. I cannot give what I do not have. Love is a power that is given first to the Lover. Love is an energy that flows from itself. It cannot flow from anything that is dead or a liar. Love is God. God is Love. He is more than the idea of Love, itself. When I do not reside and resonate within the flow of Love, I am nothing to myself. I cannot love what Love is, and not be Love also. I cannot love God and hate myself. I cannot magnify God, and despise myself, for I am a Wisdom Key from God. I am. YOU are. We are byproducts of the greatest wisdom that God has ever produced. We are his fellow Christs, in the earth. His imaginations are Christ energies, living abundantly on Planet Earth! Without Love, there is no Power, for Power is Love. Without Love, there is no Purpose. No Plan. No nothing!

We are not doing the Will of God "a favor" by despising ourselves. We are Glorious Glories of God, and to deny that, would be a lie! We have become tolerant of living a lie in order to protect God from "losing His Glory!" Listen, glory cannot lose itself! It is what it is. When we deny ourselves the Glorious Affirmation of being sons of God, our Soul will react in total desperation. It will begin to "kick over chairs, leave open perfume bottles, while positioning the laptop near a sink that's full of water," within our Spirit and Consciousness! It will cause us to lose the beautiful aroma and scent of Victory, while daily endangering our confidence and grace with the fear of disappointing the Lord we say we love! The fear of letting someone down will become too much to bear. And this whole, crazy feeling, is a result of denying ourselves a full residency of Divine Nature!

Where do YOU reside? Where do you live, within YOU? What is your Place of Residence? It is impossible to return to a Place that you know not of. The Soul will constantly give YOU a picture of its fulfillment, joy, and happiness. Have YOU seen it yet? What did it show YOU? Are you confused between the revealing of the Soul "and the mixtures" of your own, satisfaction? Can you tell the difference between a Vision from the Soul's yearning and your own, self-convenience? We usually know the difference within ourselves. We know when we are rising to the occasion or subjecting ourselves under the radar. We know the difference between standing up and sitting down. Our Soul knows when have become tolerant in existing in a lie. As we love ourselves back to Power, we are actually loving ourselves back to God. We are loving ourselves back into the Imagination of the Fullness of God. There is no Power without Originality. As we return to our Authentic Design, the flow of Power will become inevitable. We will experience the truest sense of Rest, in God. Rest is to be free of the obligation to respond to everything I perceive or see, while not calling for me, personally. If the issues are not "asking for me," I do not have to respond out of obligation. I do not have to subject myself to a death not designed for me. I do not have to be "the goodness" that someone else bestowed upon me. I do not have to live in the box "that someone else designed around me." I am free to be all that I am, wherever I am, and whenever I AM! I will live the goodness I see within me. The tone of our authenticity will speak louder than the tone of our very own voice. We will find ourselves "living our Love loudly!" Have you ever lived your Love "loudly" before? Are you doing it now?

The tone of my life is aligned with the pitch of my Soul. Many will find your "liberty" discomforting. It's cool. You are not designed to please the outside world. YOU are pleasing your inside world, which in turn, will reestablish your "outside world!" Confidence empowers YOU to live your Love at its Loudest! Don't turn down your Love for "haters!" Don't turn down your Life out of fear of being misunderstood. Those who do not know love, will never understand Love. Don't live to be understood. Live because YOU are Alive!

The Deeper we move in our Divine Love, the more the Soul will reveal its admiration of YOU. Have you realized that your Soul admires YOU? We are the nature and reflection of God. Our Soul responds to us as it responds to God. It cannot hear any vile thing concerning YOU. When we are in despair, or ashamed of ourselves, we can always imagine Life going the other way. We can always reimagine ourselves getting out of trouble. If your Soul hated YOU, it would not afford YOU with the ability to reimagine your Life. The imagination of the Spirit affords us with the possibilities of inner hope. We can think ourselves out of the prisons of our spirit. We can be free. Once the Soul reveals "The Way," take it! When we fear The Way, while yet imagining possibilities, we become illegal procrastinators. Imagination requires us to honor what it reveals. When the Soul desires to live through YOU, it will reveal the Path of the Divine to YOU. A highway shall be revealed, so walk therein; *(Jeremiah 6:16, The Scriptures)*

The "old paths" are the Original Way to Divine Life. It is not a ritual, neither is it a religious thing. It is The Origins of your Being. Life, absent of the meaning of its Being, will never find fulfillment in anything else. It can only find fullness within the Thought that produced the energy and power of its reality. It may be convenient toleration in other things, but it will not experience fulfillment. Fulfillment is an encounter with the yearning of a thing. If we encounter anything other than what we yearned for, it simply "slowed us down without overwhelming our hearts!"

We cannot afford to exist while being "slowed or weighed" down. We cannot afford to be late any longer when it comes to self-realization. We cannot afford to "see the picture" perfectly, while at the same time, lacking Clarity on how to reproduce what we've seen! This is torment. To see and not become. To see and not know what it is we are seeing. To be blind, while seeing perfectly. This is a lake of fire. This is what it feels like to not have "permission!" The mischievous child of the Soul will annoyingly "blot our names out of our Life's Permission" in order to regain our truest attention to what is truly important! Believe me when I tell you, I am not blaming the soul for anything. I know that it appears that I am speaking of the soul as some sort of "mismanaged child, looking for love and attention." But the truth is this, when we are absent of Love for ourselves, and I am not merely speaking of the idea of acceptance of ourselves, but the innate, authentic celebration of our Divine Identity. The type of celebration found in an unforced response to the appreciation of being a "clone of God!" When the Soul recognizes this reality, how will it naturally cause us to behave? When we are filled with an identity that is an "after-thought," we will not celebrate it, neither will be honor it! A life that is considered as an "after-thought" to our own selves, will destroy our confidence and power. Do you consider yourself as an "after-thought?" As an "oh, hmm?" Have you ever done something that you felt was important, and the response from another was "oh, huh?" As though everything else was more important than your obvious achievement. When what is obvious is treated in an insignificant manner, you will find yourself not wanting to share your heart with the insignificance. Imagine feeling this way about yourself. When we feel this way about ourselves, our Consciousness will refrain from sharing its Dreams with us. It will refrain from sharing Us, to ourselves, leaving us absent and void of the feelings of accomplishment.

Inspire your Soul to share with YOU. When we authentically return to Love, all of the Secrets of our Soul's desire will be revealed to us. God is not holding anything back from us. We are holding Life back from us when we fear being ourselves. When we are embarrassed to BE, out loud, the Soul will be embarrassed to share our own lives to us. It will not reveal what we are afraid to BE. Our Soul does not want to experience us retreating from ourselves. We are the Spirit of our lives. We do not merely "have a spirit" on the inside of us. We are already "inside of us," living on the outside of us. We are the expressions of our own Soul. When we return to Power, there will be a continual Manifestation of Celebration affirming the realignment of the Soul, Spirit, and the Body!

When our Body, Soul, and Spirit lacks alignment, it can only leave us open to desperation and poverty. Oneness transcends "closeness to God." Oneness IS God. In fullness. In Time. In the NOW! Closeness to God is still too far. We are not designed to stand next to God. We are designed "as God, in God, and from God!" To return to power is to evict ourselves from the convenience of spiritual "closeness." Transformation does not come as a result of being "close." It is the result of BEING, itself. Oneness as God is the fulfillment of the Christ parable of "the Vine and the Branches!" The name of the "tree," if you will, is called GOD. We can no longer afford to strive for the convenience of a cordial, tolerant, co-existence between who we truly are, and who we perceive is more "safer and easier" to accept.

Returning to Power is the greatest confirmation of Authenticity. The truest expression of the Divine will be uncovered to YOU. Comparison will no longer be "a god' to YOU, while leading you to an "illusion of anointing and spiritual power," while obligating you to a form of spiritual grandeur. When we become ourselves again, we will finally be free from the obligation to "many!" The Soul will no longer hold you in contempt, jealousy, envy, or guilt, to any other human being. The Affirmation that you once sought through these obligations, were but mere "attention seekers" projected within you through your attention seeking Soul! What we are perceiving to need from others "are simply desires that our Soul has for us!" Amazingly beautiful. The Soul will draw you unto itself, at times when you are seemingly "yearning for someone" for yourself. Loneliness, at times, is a calling from the Soul, and not a call for someone outside of YOU. When we are not a Peace with who we are, we will not have Peace where we are. When we have yet to realize the presence of our Presence, we will feel as though we are orphaned, and left alone in this world to die.

Honoring Our Presence is a divine right and permission. To honor our presence is to authentically sense that we are existing as "the literal Presence of God." We are the works of His Hands and the living testimonies of His Mind. We are the feelings and behaviors of His Thoughts. We are the movements of His movements. We treat ourselves to the degree that we perceive this truth (or not). If we feel that it is somewhat arrogant, prideful, or egotistical to feel this way, then we will intentionally hold ourselves back, no matter how much the Soul is compelling us to step up our game! We are designed from Honor, to honor the brilliance of God found in our very own workmanship. As we respond to this brilliance, we find ourselves living effectively, successfully, and abundantly. Our innate response of celebration, as a result of being an offspring of the Most Incredible Mind in all of the Universe, is enough to launch us into the fullness of our lifetime.

When we have lost our way to Divine Response, we become obligated to react to death rather than to life. We see "death" and limitation in our perspectives, more than we see Possibility and Opportunity. When we are fulfilled truthfully, we will live truthfully. Wherever authentic gratification is absent, flattery will awaken. Flattery has been the "energy of many" who have lost their way to Self. Seeking the resurrection of their lives through the validation of respected ones, while dying at their own hands, within the confines of their own spirit. To live in Honor, is a courageous thing, simply because it's a natural thing. It's the right thing to do. Living in Honor of who we are, is celebrating the Wonders of God. When we see ourselves, do we sense a spark that we are looking at God? If we are beholding anything other than the beauty of God, we are beholding an illusion. When the Soul is playing tricks with our confidence, it will present us with an illusion and stir up dissatisfaction within ourselves "until we return to the Father's Original Intent!"

The Original Intentions of God are also the Intentions of our Soul. Our Soul is being what God already is being. In real time. The Soul isn't Christian, even as it emulates everything Christ is being. Our Soul does not respond to religion. It responds to sameness and oneness. It responds in Celebration as a result of being a moving thought of the

Divine. As God is, so is the Soul. The Soul is a celebrator of the Mind and Power of God. The Soul is a navigator within the Father's Intellectual Sphere of Influence. In other words, "you have the permission to freely travel the Heart of God!" (I know, too dramatic). The Soul compels us to live in the Power of Knowing, and not the convenience of mere "believing." When we KNOW, we have fully released ourselves from the energies found "in pulling the narrative" towards our own expectations. We are no longer "pulling hope" our way, as though it will pass us by. We are living within the Power of the NOW! Living, thriving, and knowing that we are fully seen, affirmed, and necessary, in the earth. And especially necessary to ourselves, from ourselves. We are not living, missing from our own Presence. We are not hiding from ourselves as though we are a "big sin" unto ourselves. We are living our Love at its loudest! And we are annoying the fears that we once carried with us as a friend!

RECOGNIZING
SELF-EMBARRASSMENT...

Where we "are" determines "Where" we are. I didn't realize this when I was a young child. We live, carrying severe misinterpretations of identity. Even when all that LIFE required of us was to watch cartoons on a Saturday morning and mow the lawn when we are done. How we perceive ourselves inwardly will either prepare us for the future, or create the traumas that we will sift through daily as we grow into adults. Where we are determines the location of our soul. It determines "the place" from where we exist and perceive everything around us, (which in fact, is everything within us).

Our Soul is more than a spiritual analogy. Our Soul is the core of everything we are being. Our Soul is the navigator to every dimension we visit in Consciousness. It is the "data base" of everything we are, once were, and seek to be. But what happens when our Soul is desperately seeking after our attention? Did you ever think that your Soul possesses a personality unto itself? Do you think that I'm simply making this up simply for the case of interpretive literature? Our Soul responds to no one else but us. It's say tp bypass this reality, simply because where we are "determines where we are," in the way we perceive our own worth, value, and relevance to the entire scheme of the Universe.

Our Soul constantly releases information within the cores of our Consciousness, that reflects the authentic worth that we innately feel about ourselves. It releases either strength or weakness to the bones. Inspiration or desperation to the heart. As we think, so are we; *Proverbs 23:7 (The Scriptures).*

We treat ourselves as we perceive ourselves. We procrastinate with ourselves when we fear being "on time" for ourselves. Maybe, we are late for ourselves simply because we innately despise showing up and seeing no one there to celebrate our arrival! If we are too early, we will totally brunt all of the shame of being alone. These are the inward wars within the soul. The silent terrors that disguise themselves as we raise families, go to work, and get incredible advances on our jobs! These are the wars that we ignore, as we seek validation for our life's choices in the world.

Many of us have lived entire lifetimes, Inwardly embarrassed at the very thought of our own Sacredness. We feel awkward at even identifying ourselves with the term. We feel exposed and outdated, when it comes to identifying with the very agreements of our Divine Soul. As we live, in disagreement with the Power of our Soul, we will find ourselves experiencing constant dysfunctions of roller-coaster style relationships and life situations. Inwardly embarrassed at the thought of being someone "whom the Universe would readjust its schedule for!" Would the Atmosphere consider me, and grant me an audience with her Time? The fear of being considered "important enough" is enough to paralyze any dream, of any size.

Our Soul constantly yearns for us to perceive ourselves higher, and to connect on its frequency. We are not going to "fall down in shame." The more we are deficient in Oneness with ourselves, the more we are not going trust ourselves. It is imperative for us to overcome our own wealth of Goodness. This Power is not for us to borrow when times are rough. It is for us to consistently live from for the rest of our lives. We must destroy and rid ourselves of this radical co-existence between carnality and spirituality. We find ourselves adoring this hidden, flexible option of living that grants us the capacity to "code shift" our lives to appease various elements of our indecision. We are afraid to "cut off" certain elements that are responsible for "pouring into" those troubled times in our lives. We are ashamed to be seen in a state of Wholeness, out of fear of being left alone. We must recognize what it is we are fearing as a result of evolving into a more authentic expression of ourselves. The more that we are perceive that we are trying to represent a Life that has not fulfilled us, the more embarrassed we will feel trying to do so. We are only ashamed when it seems that we are being held accountable in taking on the responsibilities of a lifestyle that hasn't produced any kind of authentic satisfaction not coerced by any thing that we have done. When sensing these feelings, we silently "pull away" from being drawn to the front of the line. We find it necessary to protect our false humility at all costs. We are being compelled to realize our innate, Sacred Truth. Yet, we seek to protect our convenient truth, a reality of self-imposed satisfaction. We are caught in the middle of two opposing truths and realities. Each one desiring our full attention and companionship.

Are you fearing your ultimate perfection? Are you afraid of the term? Do you feel that you are being obligated to perform more perfectly? Are you afraid that you will fail? Are you seeking to compromise the potential of your life in order to water down pre-determined expectations? Have you determined how far you are willing to go? Do you feel the fear of being pushed by others to go further? Are you afraid to let them down? By the way, who is "them?" The Soul is not in any sort of competition with us. The Soul knows how we are designed and made. It also knows how we have also self-designed ourselves. It knows how we have intentionally "rearranged our perfection" in order to fit our convenience. We are already "perfect for our established zone of influence!" We are perfectly formed, perfectly made, and perfectly established for the world we were created for. Our emotions however, were not created. Our emotions are determined from the way we perceive ourselves "in our world!"

Worthy of Worth?

I was a very inquisitive child. I was always asking questions simply because I wanted to know where things came from, how they worked, and why they were made. I was also inquisitive about people and behavior. I guess I annoyed many that were close to me when I did this. Maybe I asked at the wrong time. Sometimes, after I would ask a question, I would get the reply "I wasn't thinking about that," as though you had to already be thinking about what I had yet to question you about. I began to measure my worth based on how much patience was rendered to me by another. If you didn't have time for my questions, I assumed you didn't have time for me. I perceived that wherever patience was rendered, value was also given. Wherever impatience resided, value was absent. I felt that my worth was based on how others would readily provide me with an intentional, listening ear. I've experienced a tolerable ear, you know, a certain degree of space that was reluctantly provided, but not intentionally and with influence. I felt like I had to hurry up with the main question, while leaving out the true yearning of my need. I was constantly left feeling in want, to the point I began to feel that this "was my assigned burden or lot in life." I began to sense that maybe I am not worthy of worth. I was good enough to be included in someone else's time or need. But, I did not receive the same strength when my presence needed it. I had to be satisfied with being included in the show for others to display. When it was my turn, I wasn't able to have all of the pieces available so, I had to prepare myself to be deficient in my presentation. I had to do what I could with the little that I had and learn to preestablish an excuse to compensate for the lack. This may sound like simple, mental issues of an inferiority complex, yes. But this "complex" is different when the war is internal. When this torment is being produced by a Soul that sees you as the most Perfect and Powerful individual in its world, the reality becomes a much different thing. YOU were thinking that the issue was merely between your body and other bodies, when in fact, the issue was between your Soul and YOU! YOU are the object of desire in the eyes of your Soul. Your Soul sees you as a brilliant creation. But when the worth your Soul perceives of YOU is not recognized by YOU, your very own life will turn against YOU. You will not readily discern how to fix it, simply because you will feel that the issue is with others and not your own heart.

The fear in perceiving our own excellence can be a daunting task. We must embrace the legal right to free ourselves from a spirit of what seems to be a justifiable, self-abasement. We must find the strength to declare this particular mindset as "inhumane" to our personal welfare. We must overcome the timidity of living as a legal, powerful Spirit in the world without feeling that someone, or some "thing," will come along and pull the rug from under us. Thus, sending us back to reality. And speaking of reality, it is imperative for us to live with "both feet in Power" instead of "one foot in the past, while the other is in wishful thinking!"

When we fear Divine Identity, we innately grant grace to the spirit of self-sabotage, giving it the legal right to dilute the excellence of our very own minds. The mischievousness of the Soul begins to quicken even more, disturbing our most common places of inner peace. Until we are provoked to wake up from the slumber of doubt and self-hate.

WHERE
IS HOME?

When the love for ourselves is misplaced by our soul, we won't trust who we perceive ourselves to be. Clarity will not be revealed to us from within us. We will find ourselves "temporarily" believing in ourselves through our respect in someone else. We will find ourselves, needing others to believe in us, for us.

Our mischievous child, when it is yearning for authentic attention and honor, will annoyingly misplace our confidence and have us desperately seeking the attention of others to raise us back from the deadness of our emotions. But this will never work. We will soon become displeased in being codependent to the opinion of others. We will try to regain our own belief. Yet, we still find ourselves struggling with being established in it. Without authentic love, Rules become the norm. Without Love, originality becomes stagnant.

An authentic understanding of the power that resides in your own, recognition of personal relevance, will provoke "your mischievous soul" to refrain from intentionally hiding away your confidence. It will inspire your soul to align itself with the greatness you have recovered within yourself. Your soul desires to establish a beneficial covenant with you. It does not possess a desire to live against YOU!

The Wisdom of God desires for us to grow with it. God wants us to grow and expand with Him. A resistant soul will find comfort with remaining established in one thought while committing to that thought. The soul will not go where it has no desire to go. It cannot take you where you have no desire to be.

Salvation is not theological. It is simply God sending Love towards us. And when we begin to love ourselves, with the Love that loved us, we will find ourselves returning back to Power! To Originality. Our Divine Realization will no longer be hidden and intentionally misplaced by a soul that is desperate for awareness, knowing, and covenant!

Where there is no realization, there is no enlightenment! Where there is no enlightenment, there is no Light to see our way back home.

Where is "home?" Do YOU know where YOU come from? Do YOU truly know WHO YOU ARE, beyond what you "feel?" Many of us have identified with our feelings, emotions, and sensitivities and have totally ignored our Divine Identity. We've connected more with what we are feeling instead of who we are being. When we are "lost within ourselves," where do we go? Where are we placed? When we are blind to our own existence, we will seek out others to grant us an existence for us to live. We desperately desire for others to know us, but it is impossible. Especially, when we have yet to know ourselves. We find ourselves under extreme pressure to live up to the prophetic word of another, instead of living up to the Knowing of our own selves. We break under the pressures of "living the good" that others project upon us, instead of the Love we see within ourselves. Without experiencing the Powers of our own, Divine Love, we waste away daily, "while continuing to smile in everyone's face." So, we must ask ourselves this question: "WHO AM I?" Am I being drawn to my Soul through love? I know all of the spiritual rhetoric, but has it solved my yearning? Do I still need someone to blame for where I AM in the energy of my life? Once we are free, from needing others to blame, we will find ourselves on the road to Discovery!

Our Divine Soul desires us to live and become the Person that we have intimately realized ourselves to BE! Who we truly are "is always yearning to appear" in the world that we have not prepared for it. We have established relationships that will naturally reject our authentic self, simply because we have ignored the cries of our Soul. We have established a lifestyle that is fearful of our authentic self, simply out of fear of survival and the capacity to prosper. When we are not truly loving ourselves, we feel more in tune with poverty than with abundance. When we lack the celebration of our Fullness, we find ourselves honoring what is limited, while fearing what is greater! When we do not honor ourselves, we do not honor our Consciousness. And when our Consciousness is not celebrated, our Soul finds itself existing in hunger.

Do we truly desire to return to Power? I cannot command your Soul to do with YOU, "what you have no desire for it to do!" We live who we feel we are. We do what we feel we have legal right to do. Many of us are as free "as the opinions we endure." We go as far as others allow us to go. Our measure of living is determined by the allowance of another.

When the soul has misinterpreted the Divine Intention of the Christ-Mind, the yearning for it will not be powerful. We cannot be fulfilled by something merely needed, but undesired. Need requires intellectual obligation instead of one's passion of heart, spirit, and desire. When love is absent, rules exist. Where there is no Love, fulfillment becomes invisible. The mischievousness of the Soul has cheated us from the excellence of Self-discovery by hiding away the Joy of our own existence. When it seeks attention, it becomes a very bad companion. This is what happens to our lives when we have yet to discover the Celebration of it. The lack of honor in living in our own presence, severely stagnates the creative energy of the Mind. It imprisons us to live from spiritual formulas instead of authentic power!

Who, or what, is "controlling" or maneuvering our capacity to self-realize? What "eyes" are we "seeing" ourselves from?

Our realization of authentic power is a treasure we already possess within the heart. Who is helping us to see ourselves? From what vantage point are we comprehending our worth, capacity, and purpose? Have we determined where, and what home is, to us?

Are we merely intrigued by the talk of adventurous transformation, and revelatory insight? Have we designed our own "deliverance?" Or, are we preparing ourselves to release the reins of our self-illusion, and gracefully release ourselves into the Power of Divine Authenticity? The "changes" we create for ourselves, becomes the changes that we sincerely await at the door. But we ought to know that we cannot design templates for the Shift. The Shift is a Design that is empowered from its own right. We may seek to design "the savior on the white horse," but that's not the Home that's coming to restore us from the unauthorized activities of the agitated Soul. We must be set free from our self-made "freedom designs." We must realize that we did not design our Original Beginnings. It was established for us, before the foundations of the world.

Who and What, are We? When we have grown accustomed to ignoring the cries of our Soul, we will naturally "create" freedom designs, inspired by what we are craving to attract to ourselves from the outside world. The deeper our Soul is inclined to require our attention, the more we too, crave the attention of the outer-world and its affirmations. We seek the freedoms which our Soul seeks from ourselves. We are simply blind to it.

What are we afraid of? Why are we intentionally ignoring the yearning of our Soul for the Sacred? What are we afraid of leaving behind? Who are we afraid of leaving behind? The fears of who "you perceive that you'll have to live without" is simply a precursor of what your Soul is feeling regarding its relationship with YOU. Now isn't that something? Our Soul is calling for us to return to our Original Alignment of Spirit and Consciousness. That sensitivity for Change is but a silent beckoning from your own heart, to come home to it. Sometimes, when our Spirit is desiring to speak with us, we get anxious and call someone else on the phone! We are intentionally making an excuse to not honor our Presence, with our presence!

How long will you tolerate "your mischievous child?" How long will you allow it to misplace your trust, competence, and confidence? Everything YOU need is already present within YOU, hidden deep down in your daily regimen of fear and procrastination. YOU are already Powerful and Wonderfully made. But, misplaced inner-standing will not allow YOU to "understand" what you already know!

There is nothing more tragic than to exist in life, as an energy that is not fulfilled with itself. To exist as a powerless form of energy. To live as a mere form of godliness, denying its own relevance and power. When we are weak in celebrating our Divine Nature, our capacity to worship the brilliance of the Divine Mind that is found in all things, will be lifeless and void. Our ability to fully understand the seasons of creativity, governance, and intentional action, will constantly be questioned and unassured. When we have lost our way, we will be passive in all of our ways.

A misplaced Clarity will have us intrigued with revelatory knowledge, while also being absent of transformation and the becoming experience. It will have us "learning" without our yearning being fulfilled. We will become more interested in information, while yet existing within the status quo of commonness. What is it that we are so afraid of?

Are we living a life that we are actually trying to abandon? When we have injured the covenant between ourselves and our very own Soul, we will feel the division within our own spirit. Before you reach out to apologize for the offense you sense you may have caused with someone, try looking within yourself FIRST! You may have offended your Sacred Self. And it is no longer on "speaking terms" with YOU!

YOU are a temple of the Divine. YOU are a unique carrier of the Creative Force of the Universe. YOU reside within the same Universe that is also within YOU! YOU are a magnetic force of Power, walking on the grounds of Planet Earth. YOU are a force of Power that's forgotten how to love yourself in the Perfect Way. Whenever YOU disqualify your relevance, you are too embarrassed to be great.

And an embarrassed king possesses no influence, no matter how powerful the title!

THE ACTUAL EXPERIENCE..

It differs from the decree. The actual manifested frequency differs from what we speak. It's a different realm of trust to give yourself over to the uncontrollable process of a decree.

Revelatory insight is only as powerful as our innate awareness for transformation. Revelation is the ultimate door towards Change and not just a unique and peculiar way to use words of knowledge.

As the heart seeks a shift, it will draw Revelatory Insight into itself. To desire true change, in the midst of a satisfied and convenient world, is a bold move by itself.

The heart can discern when the moment of invitation has been stirred within the Soul. To adhere to it, without force or coercion, is a beautiful thing. To purposely and intentionally "shift your position of existence," is a rhythm of honor. It is a beautiful beginning to Divine Realization.

The Humility found in this transformational shift in consciousness, will not be "seen" by those who "are uncomfortable with the reality found in the Celebration of Self!" To celebrate your existence is to find it worthy of God because it *is* God. When we find our lives worthy, we lose the fear of living it. We authentically trust the Word of God that moves it. We let go of the resistance to control it, knowing that we are not going to fail.

Humility is to authentically know this. False humility is to appear as a trusting vessel, while denying the power of the trust. It is the appearance of appreciation, while yet fearing the future.

Many are living a life that they don't appreciate while presenting it as though it's fulfilling. And when you are authentically living your love, they perceive that you are lying!

To live what is not appreciated, while presenting it as assurance, enables the heart to quietly become a liar on all frequencies. The aura must be maintained in order to "gleam" of the harvests of those who are truly celebrating the Life! Jesus had disciples who were "unfulfilled students," who merely gleamed for themselves the baskets of food that would be supplied after every miracle!

A life that is constantly lied about, cannot possibly fathom the truth in The Truth. The illegitimacy of humility exposes "our supposed faith" to deeply rooted wells of torment, double-mindedness, fears, and doubts at the presence of "trials, shifts, and turns of life!" An unappreciated spirituality cannot protect the possessor from "what is perceived through the natural eyes." An uncelebrated Love will not fill the heart with trust or stability!

When we are afraid to authentically love ourselves, we find ourselves afraid of being "let down" and our hopes, dashed! We are holding out for "another type of promise and satisfaction!" We are afraid to release the "falsehoods of glory" from our grasps. We are spiritually gambling with our lives. As a result of existing in this spiritual torment, our Soul will become consistently agitated in its attempt to regain your attention. The process to enlightenment can become more and more disheartening as we continue to rely on our own strength, while embracing the convenience of a perverted life of humility. Without Love, there will be no authentic celebration of Divine Nature. The need to appease others will continue and the spiral to greater realms of unfulfillment, will be our lot.

However, this does not have to BE. Just as we constantly take chances on "toxic relationships," it is imperative for us to take a chance on the relationship between ourselves and our Soul. We must begin to see the Personhood of our Soul. It's showing us how to do it, but I believe that we have been wayward for so long that we are afraid to turn it around. Our hearts reveal the truest intent of our pursuits in life. We must begin with the purest honesty, while intentionally ignoring our fears of who, or what, can be lost through the discovery. We cannot protect what we do not own. We cannot save what we do not know. This is the realization of what it is to finally LOVE. We must determine what it is about the Divine Life that we love, and also what is despised about it. We must revisit our foundations of personal thought, both mental and spiritual. We must revisit our thoughts concerning Eternal Life,

Jesus Christ, and this Kingdom of God. We must revisit our perspectives regarding fulfillment and being an offspring of the Divine. We must revisit ourselves and what we are truly passionate about. We must revisit our personal fears, as well as memories of shame, that yet control our future. We need to ask ourselves if we are truly forgiven from ourselves. The greater that You forgive yourself, the greater you will receive God forgiving YOU. We are the actions and activities of God. What activity did you embrace in living your "pardon?" Have you authentically granted Grace unto yourself? Are you too embarrassed to take it and receive it from yourself? Are you afraid to love yourself out of the poverty of nothingness?

We usually decree a thing from a particular sphere of Consciousness, Desire, and Influence. Many can also call this place, AUTHORITY. But one thing we cannot do is this; we cannot determine the Mind within the Decree. We cannot determine how the Decree will actually think or imagine. We, who decree, may have a certain feeling of expectation when we decree a thing. But what is the mind within the command that is given? How does the

Command "imagine" in itself? The Decree has a mind of its own, even while aligning with the Will of the Decree maker! We cannot determine "how" the Decree will work, neither the extent of what the decree will touch on our behalf. We usually desire an expected end, without the full knowledge of "the unexpected how!"

As we begin to make peace with our Influence, the irritation and the toxic coexistence between us and our Soul, will begin to calm itself. There will be a new, reestablishment of trust between yourself and Clarity. Without personal trust in yourself, you will fear the guiding of your own Spirit. You'll seek for a quick answer that will not require thought and discipline. When we are afraid of ourselves, we are also afraid of our thoughts. We can't trust them. Our mischievous child has spoken out of turn so many times, while using our bodies and voices, to do so. When we have been "possessed" by the agitation of an unattended Soul, we will begin to destroy the environments that truly love us and have spoken to the best within us. It is imperative to make peace with the Consciousness and to regain the Mastery of Inner Knowing. I cannot tell you how to do it. The degree of your own love for it, will reveal the way. I cannot tell how to love what you love. No one ever has to teach us how to love what we are already loving. Many will teach us how to manipulate someone else into "accepting us." But when YOU already love something, it is already teaching YOU what to do.

Love has become such a manipulative term. A word with many definitions. I don't have a clue where YOU are in your sphere of beingness. I can only share with you the Principle and the Reality that is responsible for solving my yearning. Every yearning has an object of affection. Every yearning has a Source. If we truly listen to the cries of our Soul. It will lead us to the Source. Sadly, even though the Kingdom will always be the Answer, it's not always the solution as it relates to the yearning within everyone. We yearn for where we think we are, at the time. We usually pray to God to lead us to something other than God. Many perceive God to merely be the "Divine GPS System" to other toys in life. You know, "*ask God and He will find it for you*" type a thing.

We will love ourselves out of this false humility. We will love ourselves to the point we transcend this existence in an unappreciated Life. We must be honest with ourselves. When we don't truly appreciate this Life, we become more comfortable hiding amongst other people. We need other people to share in the non-appreciation. We are living for other people. We are too afraid to live this "unvalued life" by ourselves. We are constantly seeking fun and excitement with other people, simply for the fact that we are possessing something so unloved on the inside of us. People became our salvation. People became our God. People became our church and our family. We never emotionally connected with The Divine being our actual family. It was just another form of spiritual symbolism for some of us. People became our truth. People became our validators. People became our spirituality. The results that they experienced as a result of our advice, became our measuring stick to glory. We needed them to need us. We needed to be needed. We have lived this way for years. We have "missed' the Presence of God in our lives. We have despised our very own Presence. This is why we constantly seek out affirming individuals. We seek out those with charismatic personalities. We need others to give us a template of ourselves for us to trust in. We manipulate others to see us in a positive light. False humility. We lend ourselves over to their revelational power in order to "fix ourselves." When we are afraid to LOVE ourselves authentically, and in the Perfect Spirit, we will give ourselves over to others.

We will love ourselves out of this false light. We are coming back to ourselves. Do you believe me? Do you believe YOU?

RESTORES...

A calm and peaceful Soul, forgives. It restores. Your Soul will seek YOU out in the morning times. We usually perceive this experience as "spending time with God." This is also true. It's really your presence seeking YOU out for nurturing. YOU are not apart from God. YOU ARE A PART OF GOD! You are His nature. The reality that you did not celebrate, is seeking YOU out in the morning times. Your Soul is forgiving YOU for the forgotten times.

Let it happen.

How did you and the one you love, restore the trust? How did you restore the friendship? Or, was it so fragmented to the point of irreconcilable differences? Was the usury beyond fixing? When lies yet remain, mistrust will yet be the energy of the relationship. Have you faced yourself? What did you say to yourself? Have you reconciled your needs and yearning? Are you giving yourself space, between YOU and the offended? The Soul desires to trust YOU again. It desires to trust YOU and YOU alone. But you're going to have to listen to it, if you truly love it. When you begin to love yourself authentically, you will begin to hear your heart authentically. Rid yourself of the toxic voices that mean you harm. It is impossible to coexist with fear, passivity, and truth.

What is your Soul trying to say to YOU? Have you apologized to your existence? Have you repented to your Presence? Have you intentionally sought peace with your Presence? It seeks to restore YOU. It is seeking to restore your confidence and your celebration. It no longer desires to hide it from YOU. But once it gives it back, do not seek ways to sabotage it again. Your ways reveal the truest motives of your relationships. Relationships are not built on what is said, but what is done. You cannot force your Soul to receive YOU in a manipulative way. Your Soul knows YOU. The Will of God resonates within the very core of your being. It yearns for YOU, even when you were not yearning for it. God's Love for YOU desires you, maybe more than you are desiring it. The mixed frequencies of the Spirit are the root cause for this "mischievous child!" Oneness cannot exist with two ways. Your Soul desires to go "where your very own life has no desire to go!"

Oneness cannot exist with two ways. When the desires of the Soul are deemed irrelevant, we ignore the promptings of the Divine Consciousness. We deny our "first mind!" When the First Mind is no longer first, distractions and destruction are inevitable.

What is First desires to restore YOU. It's sending you mental notes, texts, and emails. It's revealing its intentions through nature and in your dreams. When we begin to relearn Love, we will find ourselves relearning God. We will relearn ourselves after we have unlearned shame. We are not to relearn theological references. We are relearning Truth and Authenticity. We are relearning and recognizing what Value truly is. The Power and Principle of what is First, is restoring us back to Power. Back to assuredness. Back to abundance.

We must allow the Process to continue. We must allow the low places to show itself fully. We must experience authentic dissatisfaction while answering accordingly. We must honestly weigh the scales that hold the balance concerning our motives and intent of the heart. We must face our own truths, even if they are lies. We must allow the Process to actively sort out the residues of the heart. The fear of what we may lose usually determines how we will allow the Process to live out its own laws. Love is seeking to restore your Confidence. It desires to uncover all of the places it has "hidden your blessings" in. It desires to lead you to caves you didn't know existed within your heart. It desires to restore back the Joy that was hidden within traumas that you were subjected to beyond your control. Many life experiences in our humanity have mentored us in hating ourselves. Shame and Sin has taught us how to perceive ourselves as unworthy vessels, even while prophetic promptings told us otherwise. When we don't know that we can love ourselves, in spite of, we won't love ourselves. We have condemned ourselves beyond reason. We have damaged ourselves to the point we have self-sentenced ourselves to eternal judgment and damnation. We are existing in a world between heaven and hell. We are addicted to the reality a self-imposed purgatory. Living "in between torment" is a justifiable punishment, we feel, for offending our Soul. We have created a torment that will continually judge us for the rest of our lives. This is why we feel so alone within ourselves. We have abandoned our very own Presence and told it to go away. We are yet addicted to the hearing of "the good news," simply because we have grown accustomed to its seasoning. But we do not feel that it will change or transform us. We don't think it will actually grant us mercy. We are sensing through others what our Soul is sensing through us. We look for others to seek us out when actually, your Soul is seeking YOU out. It wants to give you a message to come back home. It's a bad thing to feel that your very own Soul is deceiving you. But this is what unbelief is; " *the fear of being deceived by your own heart!*"

There is no need to live in fear of Mercy. No need to fear Love. You're not going to break it. Trust is the beginning of restoration. There is no room for manipulation, nor passivity, when you are seeking to restore trust. The offended party cannot believe in you "when you're continually choosing not to believe in yourself." YOU cannot defer the responsibility of the relationship over to the offended party. YOU must intentionally regain the Trust of the relationship, even amidst your own fears of "hidden usury."

YOU must live and process your way "through the vile and muck" found in your own mistrust and motives. YOU must navigate yourself through the fears of your own feelings and mindset. Every day and every moment will be a challenge. But if YOU love it, your endurance in the process will confirm it.

Your Soul will reveal mental pictures within YOU, showing YOU coming out of the prisons of your Mind. YOU will begin to see the Beauty in your Life again. No longer will you sense that you do not deserve the beauty that your heart is revealing to YOU. Tell the Truth to those you have offended from this mischievous child. It's hard to restore your Mind without first restoring meaningful relationships. This is why we feel ashamed in front of certain people. We feel guilty enjoying life in front of those we have offended. We don't want them to see us forgiving ourselves without asking them to forgive us also. Forgive, as your Soul has forgiven YOU. Restore, as your Soul has restored YOU.

We must be truthful and honest with ourselves if we are going to also be truthful and honest with others. This cannot be a one-sided thing. We must be intentional about it, if we are to return to Power. We cannot love ourselves while lying to ourselves.

RECOGNIZING THE
AURA OF YOUR PRESENCE

YOU are a person that You are with daily. YOU also "live from within" YOU. What do YOU sense from Yourself, after entering a room? I know that you can discern the energy in a room on certain occasions. I do know that you can discern how others are "seeing" you in a room, as well. But what do YOU sense from yourself, when you are alone? What aura or vibe do you experience? What many may call "the Presence of God," is also a vibe that exudes from your very own Presence. YOU are experiencing the energy of Yourself. It may be peaceful, calm, or chaotic and anxious. It may be fearful. It may be loving. You are experiencing the Divine Personhood of Self. As a result of being the Divine Handiwork of God, it is safe to say that you are in the Presence of the Wisdom of God "when you're sitting alone in a room!" His Presence is interwoven within every strand of your Being. God is not only within YOU, "He is YOU!" YOU are a carrier of everything God is and will ever grow to Be. As God grows, so do YOU. As God expands, so do YOU. We don't usually interpret the meaning of our presence in this way, especially if we have never loved ourselves to the revealing of this language. As we love ourselves, we will redefine ourselves. The meanings of our lives are hidden within the authentic celebration of our unique Power. As we establish a habitation with inner love, we break open the wells of Divine Revelation and Truth that reveals who we truly are to ourselves. As we are, to us, is what we see, within us. We may "wish" to be perceived in a great stature, yes. But "wishing" is torment. We are yet relying on another's viewpoint to be the catalyst and responsibility in revealing our Identity. As we love ourselves, our Identity is revealed. The meaning of who we are, must first be defined by our closest companion, The Soul. When we are lost within our own presence, the more mischievous the Soul becomes.

As you recognize YOU, you will respond accordingly. Your influence is as powerful as your own self response to your Presence. As you respond, so does everything else. We cannot expect everything and everyone else in life, to get to us in a hurry, while yet lagging in response to our own presence. We all innately live "what we mean to ourselves!"

Our lives are as excellent as the excellence we already perceive. We can no longer live as slaves to the perceptions of the outside "world!" However, if we live for the approval of that world, we will be afraid to lose it. We silently seek the validation from the world we live from. Whatever state of value that we exist from, determines the opinions that we seek and attract. If we are not living from the Divine, we will not appreciate the Divine. We love, according to the Life we live from. What "Life" has your Presence revealed to you "that you exist from?" Your Presence will always tell you where you are living. The energy that you experience daily "reveals your state of Place, always!"

Everything we desire is within. Every blessing we desire to experience is already within. Everywhere we go, and ever hope to be, is within. When we have lost our way, there are no desires for everything to be within us. We want to be the last place we look when it comes to Joy. Many feel that within them, is no good thing. When we perceive that we are no good thing, we won't "seek" our Presence for anything. We are codependent with others simply because we don't need ourselves. When we don't require excellence towards ourselves, we will borrow someone else's. And believe me, if you borrow from me, I am going to want you to "pay me back in expectations!" I want to see what you have become with me. I want to experience from you, that same energy that you borrowed from my presence. We can need others without being "needy" for them. We can live interdependent with others, while yet maintaining our own Originality and Power. Many "merge" within a relationship with others, simply to borrow a template on how to live and be. We are in relationships to imitate, instead of Translate. We are using others in order to be copies. This is when manipulation is established. When we have not recognized the meaning and aura of our own Presence, we will imitate another's. When we find ourselves going down the same Path of the one we have imitated, we will "dump it on the other side of the road and seek another willing participant!" What are YOU receiving from your own Presence? You naturally receive from the spirit of the world you are living in. You're not receiving from the information that you know intellectually. You are living from where your Soul has found substance. YOU know "your" world. Your behavior and communication abilities determine it. YOU speak and relate from where you're from. It determines the vibes that attract your "tribe." Begin to evaluate the constant conversations of those who are drawn to YOU. They speak just like YOU. YOU will experience their core values more than you experience the tone of their speech. YOU will be in the midst of their "secrets" more than you are in the midst of their rhetoric. We are drawn to sameness, not "speech and charisma!" Charisma may draw us to an interest, but when we gain access to the heart of the Object, we may find ourselves abandoning it, or keeping distance from it. Charisma is the marketing power of the Heart that speaks. We love the brilliance of the Sound but have yet to comprehend the heart that is responsible for the Sound. We love the outer rays of Glory but fear the inner translation from Glory.

How comfortable do YOU feel in the presence of those who are living their Loved Life, out loud? Do you feel worthy, or a sense of unworthiness? Why do you feel that way? We recognize the strength of our own presence, while in the Presence of those who are living abundantly in their own Presence. We may not all possess the same outward materials. But we all carry the same catalyst of confidence and love. When Love is present, there are no comparisons, even if we possess different things. When Love of Self is present, there are no competitions. We are all fulfilled together. What fulfills us are not what we possess, but Who we are possessing within. It is the Beingness of Oneness that we possess within ourselves that is responsible for lifting us above the poverty of the mind. An unlimited vault of Comprehension is ever at our disposal. We have the world we are yearning for. Your satisfaction or fulfillment is the manifestation of the world you desire most.

To speak of a Christ that is not an authentic fulfiller of life, is another form of hypocrisy. This is what makes the heart sick. Many are obligating themselves to powerless testimonies in faith, speaking of a goodness that they hope for, but have yet to personally manifest it within their soul. If Christ is not the world that you yearn for, you will not learn from it. We cannot retain information regarding a reality that we have no love for. When you fear being Yourself, you will despise the revelation of Yourself.

We must recognize the fulfillment within Christ Consciousness. It can no longer be received as an interesting rhetoric "to attract the girls!" We cannot use it to attract a positive identity from others. Is this Principle the fulfillment of our lives? We become a natural witness to those things that fulfill us. As we live, we seek the opportunity to expand its power and its reach. We seek ways in which to build its Life and its Ability. We look for ways to express the Love of our Lives. We do not sink in silence and shame when it comes to the Solver of the mysteries of our lives. We cannot, or will not, keep it a secret. When Love has healed us, we become its ambassadors. We become the voice of the One that brought us back to Power. If we are not yet brought to Power, we will not seek the baton of responsibility. We will speak up for our Healer "when we have been truly healed!"

When our Soul has experienced fulfillment, it will not let us deny it. It will not make room for anything else the is not aligned with it. It will allow us to truly recognize our very own Presence. And when we do, we will stand in awe of the brilliance of the Mind of God through us. We will no longer feel the discomforts of Being.

This Reality may be hard for some to fathom, especially those who are accustomed to "doing all of the work!" We have "learned" so much about a Divine Life that has yet to authentically fulfill us, that to hear of the powerful things that will happen, are perceived as a lie. We have learned to "hype up" a Power that has yet to manifest itself as a Power in our lives, simply as a result of not yet loving, recognizing, and celebrating our own, Divine Presence.

Living from the Blood

Many find it hard to receive the spiritual truth surrounding their Divine Life. In order to believe the Word spoken within us from God, it is imperative for us to be perfected in our Love of God. Many of us did not embrace this Divine Life for the Identify of it. We took it on in the form of an insurance payment against hell. Love of the Divine was not the catalyst for our change. Instead of resonating from the Blood, we are hiding under it as a disguise. We still perceive our ugliness while hiding under The Blood!

Instead of embracing the Divine Identify for ourselves, we look for God to be manipulated by his own Truth, accepting us in spite of ourselves, while honoring His Son's blood, in place of us. We yet feel lowly, while under the Blood. We are yet in fear, but the Blood is covering us. We are using Blood to hide from the eyes of God. We are using the Blood as an escape, instead of the covenant of Love. We are living under The Blood as a protection from God instead our permission to Purpose. We are yet feeling unworthiness, while hiding under His worthiness. We innately perceive that we are not truly desired or wanted by God. We feel that we are being tolerated by God instead of intentionally made by God. Because of this, the celebration of our own Divine Presence is hard to conceive. No matter how many times we are compelled to do so.

HAVE YOU
DETERMINED YOUR HEALER?

As we are healed, we speak. We cannot help but to flow from the Love that has healed our mysteries and our secrets. Have you determined the Source of your "healing?" Have you recognized the Source that rescued YOU from shame? Many of us are taking precautionary steps in carefully weighing our life options, yes. But have you determined the Source or Force behind your Wholeness? Is there a Power that is resurgent within YOU, that is innately revealing a healing within YOU? Or, is time taking over, enabling you to merely tolerate what you perceive that YOU will never have?

We will boldly, and with confidence, serve as ministers of our own reconciliation! When something of great value has been restored to us, the degree of the value of the restoration, will serve as the Power from which we proclaim. The strength of our Influence is determined by the strength of the Value. The greater the fulfillment, the more Powerful the Voice and the Confidence. We are as confident as the healing of our minds. Confidence is not found in skill. It is the manifestation of one's recognition of personal value. We are as confident as our own Knowingness. As we know, we flow. We are the daily expressions of what has healed us. We cannot stop speaking of it. Our creativity is more than a hobby or side hustle. It is the healing balm of our Wholeness. The Continual Vibe of Authenticity is the fulfilling truth of the Healing of our limited, Self -perspective. Many of us have careers and the financial security that compensate for the lack of truly knowing who we are. If we can afford not to know, many will take it. But you can never truly afford not to know who you are. It will demand a payment later in your life. When crisis arise, our inability to find rest and assurance in ourselves, will tell the story. We may speak "the right rhetoric," but it will not calm our nerves. We will find ourselves "reassuring ourselves that we are not afraid," but deep down, we are afraid. We are scared. Our truest life is being revealed to us. This deeper life that we may feel is personal, or globally irrelevant to anyone or anything else, is revealing itself. We are the ambassadors of the Powers that have produced our fulfilment in life, regardless of the quality. We will always speak up for our "champions" without feeling put on the spot. However, we will feel "put on the spot" if we are told to speak on behalf of something that has not fulfilled us! We will feel afraid to speak up for our hypocrisy. We can only speak what is truth to us. Many are constantly complaining because that is their truth. If we are not healed, we will not "speak" from a pure place. We may speak from an intellectual reality, but there will be no Influence present. Influence is awakened through Healing. It comes alive through The Source. I can be "healed in Consciousness," while yet being limited in physical health. Healing is not just physical. By His stripes, who we truly are, will experience healing of the Soul. But when we feel that our Soul is merely a symbol and not a Person, we will not experience this great awakening of Inner-Healing!

We are stealing positive words and trying to get paid for them. We are using "big words" that have not been produced by our own healing. We are studying subjects that we perceive are "transcending the boredoms of our spiritual understanding," and making ourselves into another thing. The Source that heals YOU will be the Source that shifts your career expression. It will establish within us a "system of governance" that affirms your Healing Power. When we are not healed, we are impatient. We will go from here to there, seeking new words, perspectives, and insights, while fearing our own, unique, unlocking of the Soul. But as I previously told you, we are the last place to look when love is absent in us.

We live and create boldly in the Spirit of the Source that healed us. We find it very difficult to flow in a spirit of hypocrisy and hype. As we flow in hype, we find ourselves under constant "attack from the enemy." But it's really not "the devil." We are under attack from what is Truth. The Truth is causing us to see ourselves when we have no desire to see ourselves. Authenticity is slapping us in the face and it is causing us to live a roller-coaster experience in hypocrisy. We are trying to live what is not real to us. That is why we constantly distance ourselves from authentic people. We need a "safe space" to breathe. We are uncomfortable portraying a healing that is not present. Unhealed minds will also find ways to accuse authentic environments of being judgmental. When healing is absent from us, we feel threatened within its environments. We feel the gulf between what we are living from, and the greater world. We desire for comfort to subject itself to us, but it cannot. The mischievous Soul torments our clarity when we ignore its cries for healing.

Have YOU determined the Source behind your "force?" Have YOU recognized the Powers regarding the momentum of your Spirit? Many will recognize your Healer through the daily energy of your existence. Your living is your testimony and not just the mere events that have taken place in your Life. The tone of your Living speaks loud, loving, and clear. It speaks louder than the words out of your mouth. Have you heard "your Sound" lately?

Your Healer will never allow YOU to feel ashamed anywhere. If you are yet feeling ashamed in beautiful places, then your "healer" has not finished the job. The True Healer will never leave you intimidated. We receive from Love, the love we are loving with. God has not given us the spirit of fear, but of love, power, and a sound mind. We receive from God, how we are loving God. If I am loving God, and yet feeling fear, then I am not loving God. If I am loving God, and yet feel anxious, weak, and double-minded, then I am not loving God. I may be "loving" an idea about God, but I am not authentically loving God. Whatever I authentically love, will fulfill me. It will leave me with no empty places.

Be free of obligatory, spiritual flattery. Begin to authentically recognizes the goodness of God within the goodness of yourself. Overcome your fear of looking at YOU with kindness. Have You treated yourself with kindness? Your Healer will allow such a thing. The more healed I became within, the more I treated myself with extreme grace and kindness. I gifted myself with patience. My Healer allowed it. My Healer called me to proclaim by its Love for me. My own love for me has empowered me to speak for Love. When we are afraid to speak for Love, we fear that our unfulfilling spiritual experience is seeking to hire us for a job against our will. Whatever it is that has not fulfilled YOU, will never "call YOU to preach or lead!" If we do feel this way, we are perceiving that God will have to "break our will" in order to obey Him. A True Healer does not do this. Whatever it is that has healed us, will call us. Everyone does not have a "Moses" experience. As Moses experienced "healing," he experienced confidence in leadership. But we aren't speaking of Moses. We are talking about YOU!

Have YOU Determined Your Healer?

As we are healed, we speak. We cannot help but to flow from the Love that has healed our mysteries and our secrets. Have you determined the Source of your "healing?" Have you recognized the Source that rescued YOU from shame? Many of us are taking precautionary steps in carefully weighing our life options, yes. But have you determined the Source or Force behind your Wholeness? Is there a Power that is resurgent within YOU, that is innately revealing a healing within YOU? Or, is time taking over, enabling you to merely tolerate what you perceive that YOU will never have?

We will boldly, and with confidence, serve as ministers of our own reconciliation! When something of great value has been restored to us, the degree of the value of the restoration, will serve as the Power from which we proclaim. The strength of our Influence is determined by the strength of the Value. The greater the fulfillment, the more Powerful the Voice and the Confidence. We are as confident as the healing of our minds. Confidence is not found in skill. It is the manifestation of one's recognition of personal value. We are as confident as our own Knowingness. As we know, we flow. We are the daily expressions of what has healed us. We cannot stop speaking of it. Our creativity is more than a hobby or side hustle. It is the healing balm of our Wholeness. The Continual Vibe of Authenticity is the fulfilling truth of the Healing of our limited, Self -perspective. Many of us have careers and the financial security that compensate for the lack of truly knowing who we are. If we can afford not to know, many will take it. But you can never truly afford not to know who you are. It will demand a payment later in your life. When crisis arise, our inability to find rest and assurance in ourselves, will tell the story. We may speak "the right rhetoric," but it will not calm our nerves. We will find ourselves "reassuring ourselves that we are not afraid," but deep down, we are afraid. We are scared. Our truest life is being revealed to us. This deeper life that we may feel is personal, or globally irrelevant to anyone or anything else, is revealing itself. We are the ambassadors of the Powers that have produced our fulfilment in life, regardless of the quality. We will always speak up for our "champions" without feeling put on the spot. However, we will feel "put on the spot" if we are told to speak on behalf of something that has not fulfilled us! We will feel afraid to speak up for our hypocrisy. We can only speak what is truth to us. Many are constantly complaining because that is their truth. If we are not healed, we will not "speak" from a pure place. We may speak from an intellectual reality, but there will be no Influence present. Influence is awakened through Healing. It comes alive through The Source. I can be "healed in Consciousness," while yet being limited in physical health. Healing is not just physical. By His stripes, who we truly are, will experience healing of the Soul. But when we feel that our Soul is merely a symbol and not a Person, we will not experience this great awakening of Inner-Healing!

We are stealing positive words and trying to get paid for them. We are using "big words" that have not been produced by our own healing. We are studying subjects that we perceive are "transcending the boredoms of our spiritual understanding," and making ourselves into another thing. The Source that heals YOU will be the Source that shifts your career expression. It will establish within us a "system of governance" that affirms your Healing Power. When we are not healed, we are impatient. We will go from here to there, seeking new words, perspectives, and insights, while fearing our own, unique, unlocking of the Soul. But as I previously told you, we are the last place to look when love is absent in us.

We live and create boldly in the Spirit of the Source that healed us. We find it very difficult to flow in a spirit of hypocrisy and hype. As we flow in hype, we find ourselves under constant "attack from the enemy." But it's really not "the devil." We are under attack from what is Truth. The Truth is causing us to see ourselves when we have no desire to see ourselves. Authenticity is slapping us in the face and it is causing us to live a roller-coaster experience in hypocrisy. We are trying to live what is not real to us. That is why we constantly distance ourselves from authentic people.

We need a "safe space" to breathe. We are uncomfortable portraying a healing that is not present. Unhealed minds will also find ways to accuse authentic environments of being judgmental. When healing is absent from us, we feel threatened within its environments. We feel the gulf between what we are living from, and the greater world. We desire for comfort to subject itself to us, but it cannot. The mischievous Soul torments our clarity when we ignore its cries for healing.

Have YOU determined the Source behind your "force?" Have YOU recognized the Powers regarding the momentum of your Spirit? Many will recognize your Healer through the daily energy of your existence. Your living is your testimony and not just the mere events that have taken place in your Life. The tone of your Living speaks loud, loving, and clear. It speaks louder than the words out of your mouth. Have you heard "your Sound" lately?

Your Healer will never allow YOU to feel ashamed anywhere. If you are yet feeling ashamed in beautiful places, then your "healer" has not finished the job. The True Healer will never leave you intimidated. We receive from Love, the love we are loving with. God has not given us the spirit of fear, but of love, power, and a sound mind. We receive from God, how we are loving God. If I am loving God, and yet feeling fear, then I am not loving God. If I am loving God, and yet feel anxious, weak, and double-minded, then I am not loving God. I may be "loving" an idea about God, but I am not authentically loving God. Whatever I authentically love, will fulfill me. It will leave me with no empty places.

Be free of obligatory, spiritual flattery. Begin to authentically recognizes the goodness of God within the goodness of yourself. Overcome your fear of looking at YOU with kindness. Have You treated yourself with kindness? Your Healer will allow such a thing. The more healed I became within, the more I treated myself with extreme grace and kindness. I gifted myself with patience. My Healer allowed it. My Healer called me to proclaim by its Love for me. My own love for me has empowered me to speak for Love. When we are afraid to speak for Love, we fear that our unfulfilling spiritual experience is seeking to hire us for a job against our will. Whatever it is that has not fulfilled YOU, will never "call YOU to preach or lead!" If we do feel this way, we are perceiving that God will have to "break our will" in order to obey Him. A True Healer does not do this. Whatever it is that has healed us, will call us. Everyone does not have a "Moses" experience. As Moses experienced "healing," he experienced confidence in leadership. But we aren't speaking of Moses. We are talking about YOU!

OUR HEALING CREATES ASSIGNMENTS FOR US

The Source that is responsible for healing us, creates assignments for us. It is responsible for our Purpose and daily navigation in life. Our Purpose is established by the healing of our Consciousness, and not just the spiritual rhetoric that we feel we have the experience to facilitate. We are imparting life, and not just facilitating a class. As the Soul restores itself back to YOU, it will reveal this Power and Reality to YOU. As YOU return to Glory, the Glorious things will also return, or be realized, by YOU. Your Purpose is found in the "space from which YOU are healed!" Your response to fulfillment will determine your assignment. Your innate response to Love, determines your place in the Earth. It reveals the Joy that is set before YOU. Where Joy is absent, shame resides in its place. We cannot prosper in life when shame is constantly speaking to our Soul. We will seek out strangers for which we will disguise ourselves in Power. But when we are in the presence of authenticity, we will appear naked and ashamed. Our Healing will perfectly position us in authority. It will not give us a false report. As a matter of fact, we are not responsible for the report, the fulfillment is. Whatever fulfills, is the report. If we are not fulfilled, then the report becomes open to every sign of distraction.

Wherever YOU are Healed, is your Command. YOU naturally command wherever YOU are Whole. Is your Presence a place of wholeness for YOU? In His Presence is fullness of Joy. We authentically vibe wherever we are the same recipients of Energy. When the Energy is One, the Fullness will not be divided. Have you determined on "whose" behalf you are speaking of today? Just thought I'd ask. The Gift you've obtained as a result of your Life being healed, has led YOU where? Did you receive this Gift as a Healer? Many are not fulfilled by their gift of salvation, simply because it was not received as a fulfiller of yearning, but an insurance policy to escape a very hot place. We received it as an intelligent, spiritual decision, but not as a Dimension of Healing for the Mind. Many feel fine "as it relates to their religious experience," but afraid as it pertains to Life. As we experience our True Source of Healing, the Mind of Christ will awaken in us. We will find ourselves sharing the same Mind as Christ. We will embody the same knowingness and energy of the Christ Person. Our Soul awaits this moment and will continue to annoy us until we listen to it.

Our Healing expands us. When we are fulfilled in The Source, we can speak and write from that Source. It's hard to write over 1000 words on something that has not produced a beautiful power in you. We struggle to articulate where translation of Spirit has not taken place. We become bound in our limitations and skill capacity when we are not yet fulfilled by Healing. We may take classes to learn new skills. But the reality of influence is awakened through the fulfillment of being Healed in the Soul. Where we are not Healed, we are not free to BE. We may speak. But we will not be heard within ourselves. We feel unheard by others simply for the reason of not being able to "hear" ourselves. YOU won't matter until YOU matter to YOU! Healing will send YOU on a great Journey within your own Presence.

Healing is your companion and friend. You are not lonely

when you are healed. You are only empty when your Soul has grown sick by exhausting its energy in its search for new strangers for which we disguise our emptiness. When we recognize our Healing Source, we become anew. We realize the potency of the original creation we have become. Without realization, unfulfillment resides.

AUTHENTICITY CANNOT LIE!

When we live, representing an unfulfilling life in the eyes of some, we sense the obligation of providing the unfulfilled with an illusion of grandeur. Creating an expectation of a greater hope that may truly never come! The heart that has yet to discover the worth and wealth of purpose, is only open to "temporal blessings and confirming signs" to carnal contentment. The seeker seeks hope in a myriad of ways and forms, simply for the reason of maintaining a type of expectation. But without a heart that yearns for the Shift, the heart of the seeker will continually grow weary. It is tolerable to "cordially accept a thing" as time progresses without actually "transforming into the essence of the thing." We may ignorantly label this progression "growth," but there is actually no growth at all. We are simply tolerating a coexistence with an unappreciative relationship that is supposed to be good for us. The Power of Authenticity is severely missing with this form of relationship.

Authenticity carries within it the influence that is responsible for your personal Shift. Influence is not how you speak. Influence is the truth of who you really are! Influence cannot lie. When the Soul has experienced a Divine Healing, we will naturally speak and flow from the Impact of this resurgent confidence. It will be more than a testimony, describing a past event of the miraculous. This Truth will be a constant flow of NOW, an ever progressive unfolding of prophetic clarity and divine influence. Your Life will experience a unique awakening of continual Power and Explanation. Your fulfillment will be experienced through a continual, evolution of Completion. Meaning, your entire life will be fulfilled, while yet moving forward into New Realms and Dimensions. Influence cannot lie and act in any other way. Influential Growth is the finality of one's "spiritual arrest of the Soul!" The Shift is more than moral, but of Consciousness. The basis from which one exists from their "new world" will be clearly seen. The Shift cannot lie. Authentic Change does not, and will not, act fulfilled. It is the Spirit of Fulfillment and the Rest from a wandering within the various options of a mischievous soul. When the Soul has found its rest, it will also rest the Body.

Authenticity cannot lie. Whatever we find pleasure in being, will be the truth that creates the vibe. The Power you desire is a result of the freedom you seek to experience. The results you desire are hidden within the Person you truly desire to be, without fear of judgment or criticism. Have you determined WHO YOU DESIRE TO BE? Whoever we decide to BE, will always be criticized by something or someone. A system or an opinion. Frequency will decide how to flow with whoever YOU decide to BE. Relationships will decide how to flow with whoever YOU decide to BE. It is up to YOU to determine what POWER is for YOU. Authenticity cannot lie. Either we find freedom within convenient Truth, or we discover Freedom within our Sacred Truth. The Divine never established the difference. Our values did. We decided that there was a difference between the two. Our own wanderings and mixtures within the Soul "created an alternative world for us to live in!"

When we confidently live within our truth, whatever we decide for it to be, Influence will arise. Whether or not this influence will help lead others to a place of

Divine Fulfillment or Solution, or lead them to a bridge of convenient satisfaction, will remain to be seen. I have discovered that we all innately know where and how we desire to live. But our fear of what will be thought of it, frightens our decision and hinders our movements toward it. We are allowing others to determine how we make up our mind about a thing. The environments of thought that we mutually share agreement with, are a constant in our conversation. We cannot flow in conversation that has nothing to do with our "secret" reality. Whatever is authentic, cannot lie. Regardless of the nature of the authenticity. We all innately know how we desire to live, as well as know the degree of Power and Freedom we wish to possess.

There is no magic to Authenticity. No sincere, mental intentions that will flatter or fool the Spirit Realm to "poof up a blessing," simply because we said the right thing or "quoted the right verse." Thinking positive does not always guarantee a sudden, positive result. Many find themselves "tempting" the atmosphere by "window shopping" multiple streams of spirituality and possibilities. The heart of the unconvinced feels more connected to "charms, codes, and potions" than an authentic shift of Life within the Spirit. When the heart is not fulfilled, the patience to Self-Discovery is perceived as an enemy rather than a friend. As stated earlier, we already know within ourselves "the reality of the life we desire to live." We have already identified within ourselves if we are seeking a life that is void of responsible discipline, influence, and principles of the Sacred. Or, if we merely desire a life that will grant us all we desire, without the process of authentic change. We desire to live well, but we have no desires to experience the pain that comes with CHOICE!

When we have yet to recover our divine love of Self, we will find ourselves drawn to many interests, but only arrested to our own kind. We will be drawn to those who are carrying a Glory that we may be interested in, while not possessing the yearning for its Fullness.

When we are drawn to "flesh," while fearing the fullness of Spirit, this confirms that it is our very own Spirit, that is yearning to speak to us. We are projecting towards another, that which Spirit is desiring to have with us. The sounds of Power are addictive to the flesh, and in some ways, climactic to the senses. Yet, to fully cross-over into Divine Oneness, is a fearful reality to the Soul. We fear the commitment to consistency, while at the same time, drawn to the sensuality of the sounds of pure hope!

This is a mental torment of duality, which is to live in various places at the same time. Double-minded-ness creates double decisions which are responsible for tearing our lives apart. We find ourselves not knowing where to go. And it's not because we don't have choice. It's because we are afraid of the consequences that come with choosing either option. Authenticity cannot lie, no matter how silent you try to hide its energies. Who YOU truly desire to be, is revealing itself. Our absence, in prominent places of Spirit, can be discerned. And our continual presence, in places of doubt, limitation, and convenience, can also be seen. We are found in the Places that "called for us, and we answered." And the only Places that seek us out are the places that we inwardly inquire about. What the heart seeks for, will soon knock at the Door. Authenticity cannot lie.

We are lonely for ourselves and have no clue. We are carrying our own Solution and have no clue.

Change will answer the invitation from your Soul. After your Soul radically "positions" you for The Return, it will suddenly surround you with a myriad of mental opportunities. The door to greater knowing appears bold, arrogant, and inconsiderate, at first appearance. It does not consider our feelings of familiarity or endearment. Change is a beautiful force that carries a frightening sound to bold, new horizons. It reveals possibilities about us that can make us laugh in unbelief. It's too positive, profound, and powerful to be our lifelong truth. We don't even look like what we are hoping for. As a matter of fact, we feel a sense of guilt for even considering that we are even close to being this Profound Person. We tend to reach for what is already conveniently relevant to not who we perceive ourselves to be, but also to what others could readily perceive us being, without giving too much thought. When I decided to run for the office of State Representatives for the Texas Legislature, many could not perceive that of me. For a minute, I couldn't see that for me as well. I am not, nor will be, a politician. But to establish a certain civil, moralistic, and spiritual approach to Humanity, which far exceeded the reality that many constituents have been known to experience. I wanted to make a change. My approach was bold, new, and different. Many "heard" my message. Yet, they were 'stuck" in that same political machine that determined a certain familiarity of the status quo. They heard something new, yes. They just couldn't find the will to totally believe it and embrace it. We feel that "new" does not always have the Power to change what has been prevalent for so many years. When we hear this profound news concerning who we truly are, we "desperately want to believe it." But our habits, emotions, and experiences have settled themselves in this space of time. Our very own lives will allow us to be "tickled at the notions" of greatness, but our "credit report" in the Spirit will deny us the approval for the loan!

To return to Power means that we will have to begin to "work on our own approval!" It is imperative for us "pay off the debts" concerning our unbelief of Self. We are going to have to "re-open the case" that ended in "judgement" and establish some sort of "mental payment plan!" It is imperative for us to shift our methods of completing tasks, communicating with ourselves, and making decisions. Intention, without execution, is nothing but a lying promise. We have lied to ourselves continually. We have given the responsibility of clarity over to the atmosphere. We are silent and hope that others "will take on the responsibility of interpreting our ways!" Well, your Soul has no desire to interpret your absence any longer. It's time to speak up for yourself. It's time to embrace the Truth of where YOU are going, once and for all!

To return to Power, it is imperative for YOU to repay your Soul for the time you've been away. Arrange to clear the debt of your arrears. You owe "back child support" for the abandonment of your Soul. Fulfillment is when we find "rest" in the right place of our lives. When fulfillment comes, it will not leave us to the discretion of another answer, another search, or another person. When we find, what our hearts have yearned for, it will not leave us open to anything else. Rest has come. When the Soul has found Rest, it will enable us to truly listen without fear of missing the mark. We can listen, without fearing that we are incomplete. We will hear, without feeling the anxiety of being lost.

When we have "failed" at trying to be "Divine," we will no longer seek to be Divine. When we have "failed" at being strong, we will no longer seek to be Strong. Whatever "good" that we have failed miserably at, is a Good that we will no longer desire to be. YOU cannot fail at who you truly are. We fail at "who we think we should be." We fail at "what we feel" we have missed. We fail at our own misinterpretation of our Divine Self. We fail at our own misunderstanding. We have not failed in the Truth. We have failed in the illusion. And illusions are good things to "fail" in because maybe, if we accept that we are no longer lies, we will finally receive the Truth about US!

That we are amazingly beautiful, powerful, and adored...

ANTICIPATION.
CLOSING ON THE LIFE...

When the heart hears of all of the possibilities of a Life not yet accepted, it creates tensions of strain, fear, and impatience. Hearing what you can do, while at the same time, not doing it, is torment. Especially, if it's not an anticipated life. When we anticipate a future Joy, we draw it closer to us intentionally. When we find ourselves not only needing our Lives back, but "wanting" our Lives back, we will create a force of attraction that will transcend obstacles, hindrances, and laws. It is as though we are in the exciting, yet tedious process of homebuying.

Before we commit to this very important decision and process, we must first realize that the space we are currently residing in "is too small or has grown irrelevant" for what we are desiring to do. Others have also come to the conclusion of being in crowded spaces. They too, have realized that the present situation is cramped. However, they have no desire to do anything different. A realtor cannot make a person into a buyer. A realtor can only guide a customer who is

110

already prepared, or has made a decision to buy. When we are ready to pursue, we seek a photograph. A tangible Vision. A model of the Life we are intentionally seeking.

There can be two beautifully single people. You can hype each party, introduce them to one another, and say that they look beautiful together, yes. But you cannot make them love one another. YOU cannot make them accept one another, no matter how cute and gorgeous they look together. We cannot make the heart LOVE. I cannot make you love yourself, no matter how powerful of a future that I see in YOU. My perceptions of YOU cannot force you out of the cramped, yet tolerable space of consciousness that you've grown completely satisfied with. The momentum to move forward is a result of not only need, but one's own adamant desire. A recognized need, accompanied with intention, creates movement. Habits are recalibrated. Relationships are recalibrated. YOU are now determining the amount of "house" you are seeking to purchase. YOU are determining the "neighborhood" that you are willing to reside in. In other words, YOU are determining the Life you desire, as well as the Atmosphere of Influence that will now become the Principle from which you will continue to exist, grow, and thrive. And because of this intention, YOU will now seek to gain "pre-approval" for your new discovery. YOU are now seeking The Source of your "New Life" and inquiring of wisdom on how to "purchase" this Divine Power. Anticipation propels us to look for our Power. The "lazy buyer" will sit back and see if everything will simply come over to them without intention. But this is not the way our Return to Power works. The Joy of the Anticipation propels us to the deep and continual search. It is as though you've embraced a "second wind of patience" that keeps your spiritual adrenaline in a consistent force of forward. You're getting close and you're getting everything together.

The Need and the Desire must come together. Need alone, will not produce a consistent rhythm. When YOU begin to see yourself from the eyes of Joy, you will begin to move with great intention towards your Decision and Commitment. The Realtor can only guide you to the Places that are already resonating within YOU. They cannot make you buy. They cannot give you finances. They establish a connection between YOU and what YOU seek. They can only negotiate the business dealings between where YOU are and where you are desiring to go. The Spirit of Wisdom will negotiate the requirements and intentions between YOU and the Source of your Yearning. The Source already desires to grant you the Promise. And when all of the details have been established, a "date to close on the deal" will be scheduled. Has your Divine Closing date been determined? YOU can see it. Anticipating a Reality that is already yours. When the "seller of the Reality" is the Source, He can shift the laws and grant it to YOU "before you sign" if He so desires. Permissions are given when the closing has been established. YOU will create miraculous movements when Closing is inevitable. In our own personal experience, we were able to "move in our home" two weeks before we closed on it. The Seller allowed me to take down the FOR SALE SIGN. The Seller granted us certain permissions, simply because the deal was already DONE! When everything has been settled in the Atmosphere, the other things must realign and recalibrate themselves. The Seller can shift the law of a thing to accommodate whom they have specifically favored. When

YOU rediscover Yourself, there will be Divine Favor given to YOU. The Spirit has the Power to grant permissions to the pursuer. When the Commitment has been realized, settled, and approved, begin to expect a new shift in the laws of things. When the love for ourselves have been proven authentic, YOU will find yourself creating New Movements in your life. YOU will boldly go Places you have never gone before. POWER happens when we no only realize our need for it, but also our earnest desire to Become it. Without desire, there will be no Purchase.

I cannot make a "believer" believe. But YOU can help your belief. YOU have the power and permission to fuel your knowing. It all comes with your own recognition of a cramped Spirit and Soul, as well as your self-intention and desire to GET UP AND LEAVE!

Have YOU ever wanted yourself in this manner? Have YOU ever experienced an excitement concerning your own life? We all have experienced excitement about a certain thing being given to us or even afforded to us. But have YOU ever experienced Divine JOY simply from the

Presence of YOU? This is the Power that we so desperately miss regarding ourselves. It would also be safe to say that this is a reality that many of us ignore. But it doesn't have to be YOU, anymore.

LOVE wants YOU to occupy the Vision that you seek within. LOVE will shift the Law of Time in order for you to experience what you've already occupied within your spirit. LOVE will grant you the desires of your heart, once you make residence in it before YOU obtain it. LOVE yourself, until your Vision returns to YOU. LOVE your mind back to YOU. LOVE your confidence back to YOU.

LOVE You, back to YOU!

WHO WE ARE
WILL LET US KNOW

Who we are will surely let us know. It will show us. It will take us there naturally in our hearts and not by way of the noise. It will take YOU everywhere The Divine has spoken. You won't hear this from your ears. You will know it through your Soul and Spirit. In the silence of divine confidence, YOU will sense the unction of Becoming propelling you forward. Our origin and design will naturally place us in our life's position. We won't have to ask for it. It will happen naturally. It won't happen merely because I've written it. It has happened in me, therefore I am sharing it.

When YOU arrive to the "place of trust," YOU will find yourself relinquishing the controls to your emotional response to Change. This can be a very touchy issue, seeing that certain People desire the right and privilege to do with their emotions and feelings as they please. Those who desire to make excuses will be offended by those who declare their ability to win! When we have yet to gain self-trust in our own stability, we will harbor resistance against "the New

Beginnings!" Conquering this illusional mindset is your choice and your choice alone. Your ability to experience this "breath of Divine fresh air," is completely up to YOU and your endurance.

Give yourself and your Soul the love you need from others. if others are needed to inspire you to love yourself, you will despise yourself for the rest of your life. You will grow more and more afraid of being "alone! Loving yourself the least, will naturally make you "toxic," to your own self. The less that you love yourself, the more it will cause you to drain the Love that others are already giving you. You're going to pull for more and more "energy" from what is already authentically being given. It will never be enough. You will always complain. Until you begin to do your own self work, and self-love, you will continually feel empty, tired, and invisible.

A toxic relationship is not between you and another person. It's between YOU and the lack of authentic love and power that you are experiencing within your own Presence! A "self-toxic" individual will intentionally "puncture holes within their own consciousness," allowing them to severely waste their previous encouragement.

Toxic people will never "save the deposits of love" that they've already been given. They simply count the amount of "pours" that's been supplied, for personal validation. When our love is low, it is a reflection of the absence of dialogue and nurturing between our own Soul and ourselves. We must find the Treasures that we believe in and begin to "water those Seeds of emerging love" that we are progressively recognizing in ourselves.

Change is not impossible. Change will happen at our command, in our time, and in our own desire. Change is the beginning key to Transformation. Many desire for change to happen, minus becoming anew. As long as we exist from a convenient, yet limitational core value, our capacity to make empowered Decisions will be non-existent. We cannot decide beyond our ability or willingness to live. We will not make a decision beyond our own, familiar comfort zones. We may desire for the Atmosphere to act or respond differently, but it will not. LIFE responds to us in accordance to how we respond to our selves. Change, in all things, must begin in our own house.

If we are to return to Power, we must intentionally move beyond a settled understanding of truth. Understanding, and Transformation, are entirely different things. Just because we comprehend the correlation between certain examples, gestures, and symbols, does not necessarily mean that we are yearning for Transformation. Many "understand," while yet holding on to the familiar, with dear life. Change is a gift that the Seeker grants themselves. It is the application of the Secrets of life, in which YOU find most pleasing.

The Image that Pleases YOU!

Along with Vision, comes strategies for Change. Vision "is an Image that pleases YOU!" It is an outcome that produces excitement and inspiration. It is an image that establishes curiosity and desire. If it pleases you enough, it will arrest your attention and focus. It will give YOU new things to speak and say. It will inspire YOU to inquire of new habits and activities. It will make YOU say, "What do I need to do to get this or that?" If it arrests YOU correctly, it will hold YOU in place. It will settle YOU. Have YOU experienced this "image that pleases YOU?" Do YOU believe that it is yours? Do YOU perceive that God is going to take it away from YOU? Have YOU determined the worth of this "image?" Is it a responsible image? Is it a self-serving image?

You see, Change can go both ways. Many desire change for common, limited, and carnal reasons, while others seek Change for profound, responsible, and powerful reasons. Change is an Image from the Values of the Heart. As the heart "legally perceives itself to be," so will our natural and spiritual perspectives be. Change cannot be told. It is an invitation to the heart, based on the Image that Pleases us. If it's pleasing to YOU, "IT WILL TELL YOU WHAT IS NECESSARY TO MAKE IT HAPPEN!"

How pleased are YOU with your existence? How pleased are YOU with "knowing YOU?" Have you determined if your presence is worth knowing by YOU? Well, if you want it to be, It surely will be. And always remember, "our lives will take us wherever we feed it." Wherever we entertain it. Wherever we nurture it. Wherever we dialogue with it about. Whatever we feed it, will need us.